John Hedgecoe's Darkroom Techniques

Edited and designed by Mitchell Beazley International Limited
14-15 Manette Street, London W1V 5LB

© 1985 Mitchell Beazley Publishers
Text © 1985 Mitchell Beazley Publishers and John Hedgecoe
Photographs copyright © John Hedgecoe 1978, 1979, 1980, 1982, 1983
and 1984

First Fireside Edition, 1988
Published by Simon & Schuster Inc.
Simon & Schuster Building, Rockfeller Center
1230 Avenue of the Americas, New York, New York 10020
FIRESIDE and colophon are registered trademarks of
Simon & Schuster Inc.

10 9 8 7 6 5 4 3 2
10 9 8 7 6 5 4 3 2 1 Pbk.

Library of Congress Cataloging in Publication Data
Hedgecoe, John.
    John Hedgecoe's Darkroom techniques
    Includes index.
    1. Photography — Processing. I. Title.
II. Title: Darkroom techniques.
TR287.H35   1984   770'.28'3   84-5457
ISBN 0-671-50890-3
ISBN 0-671-66442-5 Pbk.

Typeset and prepared by T&O Graphics and
Taylor Jackson Designs Ltd, Lowestoft, Suffolk
Reproduction by Gilchrist Bros. Ltd, Leeds
Printed and bound in Portugal by Printer Portuguesa, Sintra

Editor	Frank Wallis
Associate author	John Farndon
Consultant art editor	Mel Petersen
Art editor	Zoe Davenport
Production	Jean Rigby
Artists	Stan North, Sandra Pond, Kai Choi, Kuo Kang Chen

THE WORKBOOK OF DARKROOM TECHNIQUES

JOHN HEDGECOE

A Fireside Book
Published by Simon & Schuster Inc.
New York London Toronto Sydney Tokyo

CONTENTS

INTRODUCTION

Photographic creativity does not end in the split second that the shutter is open. True, there is not much that can be done to make an arresting image from a picture that was taken with a maximum of error and a minimum of flair: the more technically competent you are in handling your camera, the more you develop a painter's eye for form, tone, composition, color, mood and atmosphere and, most important of all, the idea behind the picture, the more successful you will be. But a great deal of the

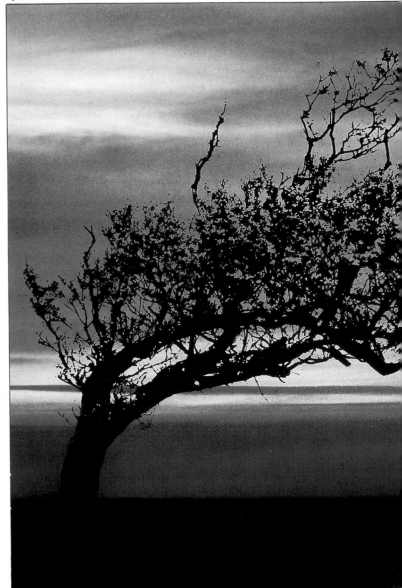

pleasure in photography, as well as a considerable stretch of the path to success, begins only when the film is removed from the camera. The darkroom is a kind of alchemist's laboratory, where the base metal of the prosaic can be turned into the gold of the unusual, where mistakes can be rectified, reality manipulated and your personal vision given full expression. The following pages introduce some of the bewildering range of techniques you can use to achieve those ends.

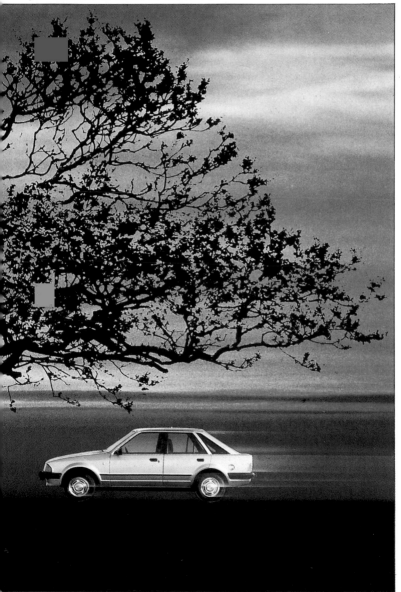

THE DRY AREA

You don't need a proper darkroom for any of the techniques described in this book. All can be attempted successfully in an improvized darkroom in a bathroom, bedroom or garage. But even if your workspace is makeshift, your organization must not be. Disorder does not stop you getting results, but it can stop you getting first class results. Plan the layout of your darkroom carefully, separating each operation as much as possible. The most important division is between the 'wet' bench where chemicals are used and the 'dry' bench for all procedures that do not need chemicals such as enlarging.

The illustration below shows one possible way of organizing a dry area. It is designed to face the wet bench layout on the following page. Very few items of equipment are absolutely essential, except for the enlarger, but you will find things like scissors, tape, scalpel and rulers far more useful than you ever imagine. The pinboard keeps them easy to hand, and easy to put away, in the neatest possible fashion. Notice how the safelight is mounted over the cutting board, where you need to see well.

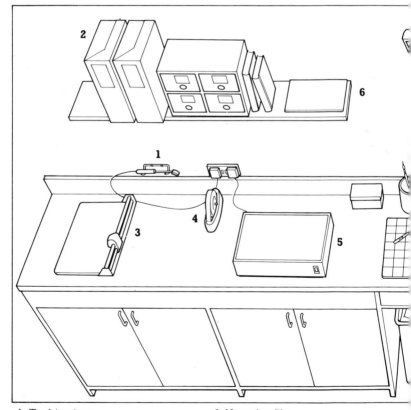

1. Tacking iron
2. Files and records
3. Print trimmer
4. Masking tape dispenser
5. Light box
6. Negative file
7. Safelight
8. Pinboard
9. Retouching brushes
10. Rulers, scissors, tape, notepad

● **If space is restricted** and you can't arrange separate wet and dry benches, divide the printing and processing areas with a vertical partition or splash board to protect the enlarger and paper.

● **Raise the enlarger** on an improvized plinth if space is so restricted that you cannot even erect a partition to separate it from the wet bench. This helps to keep splashes off the enlarger baseboard. Be sure that the enlarger is supported firmly, though

● **Electrical equipment** should be in the dry area unless, like tray warmers and motorized processors, it is designed for the wet area and has the necessary safety features.

● **Mount the sockets** for the enlarger, meters and so on, conveniently at bench height.

● **Paint the wall** behind the enlarger matt black to cut down the effects of light spilling from the negative carrier. Paint the rest of the darkroom white for maximum light.

● **Mount shelves** above both wet and dry benches to keep small items of equipment readily to hand. Round off corners and don't mount shelves near the enlarger — it is easy to bump your head.

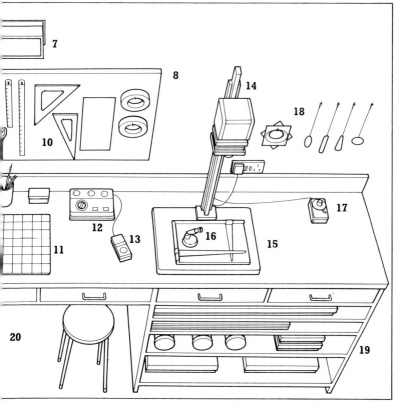

11. Scalpel and cutting board
12. Color analyzer
13. Meter probe
14. Enlarger with color head
15. Easel with adjustable masks
16. Focusing magnifier
17. Exposure timer
18. Printing masks
19. Storage space for print paper
20. Waste bin

THE WET AREA

All the processing and chemical mixing should take place in a separate wet area. You can get special processing sinks, made of polypropylene, PVC or glass-fiber. These contain all spillages well and are easy to wash down after processing. Nevertheless, if you are careful, you can get away with processing on a flat bench, providing the sink is reasonably nearby and the area is well cordoned off. Cover the surface of the bench in plastic laminates to protect it from chemicals and erect both a splashback to protect the wall and a rim at the front.

The illustration below shows one possible way of organizing the wet bench. It is designed to face the dry bench on the previous page. The processing sequence would normally run from left to right along the bench. Prints come from the enlarger on the left, into the developing tray, into the wash tray and fixing trays, arranged in a row along the bench and then into the sink. This arrangement suits most right-handed people. Left-handed people may prefer to organize the bench in the opposite direction.

1. Graduates and measuring jugs	6. Spirals
2. Funnels	7. Tray warmer
3. Thermometer	8. Print tongs
4. Sponge	9. Print processing tube
5. Film-processing tanks	10. Safelight with string pull

● **If space is very restricted,** you may be able to arrange the three trays needed for black and white print processing in a tier on shelves.

● **A water supply and sink** are not absolutely essential, since you can keep fresh water in gallon tanks and take films and prints out to a sink. But having water on tap and a place to drain solutions makes life infinitely easier.

● **A bright safelight** over the wet bench is essential. You need to see clearly for black and white printing in particular.

● **Arrange the switch** for the main room light on a string pull easily accessible from both wet and dry areas. The string means you can switch it on even with wet hands.

● **Ventilate the area** around the wet bench properly.

● **Store chemicals** well away from the dry area of the darkroom.

● **With a light-tight print tube** you can even process prints without a proper wet area; an ordinary sink will do. But if you process prints or films in the kitchen sink, be sure that chemical spillages cannot contaminate food or eating utensils.

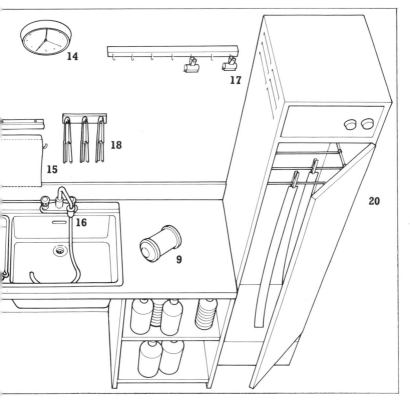

11. Process timer
12. Storage space for trays
13. Ventilation fan
14. Clock with clear face
15. Paper towels
16. Water filter
17. Clips
18. Squeegees
19. Draining board
20. Film-drying cabinet

ROUTES TO THE PRINT

The plan on this page shows the major steps on the route to the final print using each of the three main types of film: black and white film, color negative or print film, and color slide or reversal film. In each case, the first step is the same, entailing loading the exposed film into a lightproof processing tank.

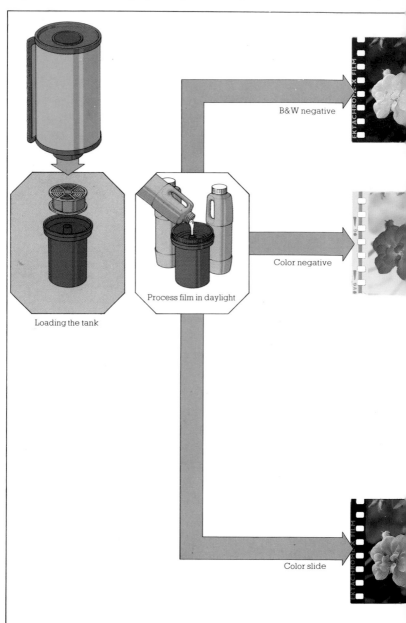

B&W negative

Color negative

Process film in daylight

Loading the tank

Color slide

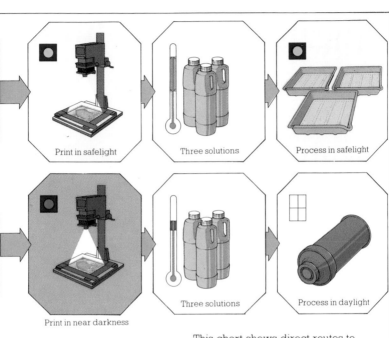

Print in safelight   Three solutions   Process in safelight

Print in near darkness   Three solutions   Process in daylight

This chart shows direct routes to the print, but there are many other possibilities. For example, by copying a slide onto negative film, you can make a print using negative paper, which is cheaper than the reversal paper used for making prints from slides. It is possible to make monochrome prints directly from color negatives, and, by copying, from slides.

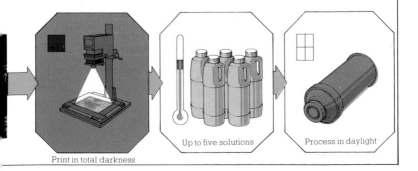

Print in total darkness   Up to five solutions   Process in daylight

13

CHANGING THE IMAGE

A photographer often feels the need to manipulate in some way, even if only to crop to improve composition. Manipulation can be as simple as correcting perspective in the enlarger or as complicated as dye transfer: you can partly change an image or create an entirely new one. The chart below shows the main ways of manipulating the image.

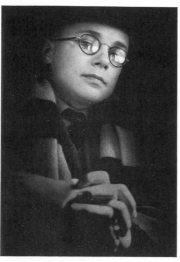

Local exposure control
By using masks to cover certain areas of the print during exposure, you can exert very precise control over the final appearance of the picture. Techniques include: burning-in (page 58-9); dodging (60); contrast control (61); vignetting (62-3); perspective control (64-5).

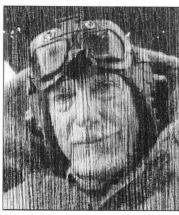

Texture effects
You can give prints a different 'texture' in a variety of ways: by printing on different types of paper (glossy, smooth, matt, eggshell and so on); by covering the print with texture screens during exposure (88-9); and even by making prints on a variety of surfaces (112-13).

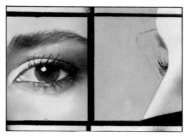

Print finishing
Even the finished print can be manipulated in a variety of ways. Prints can be retouched to disguise blemishes or to repair defects (104-5); colored by hand with dyes and paints (106-7); spray-painted with an airbrush (108-9); and dipped in toning baths to change their color completely (110-111).

Separation techniques
Many effects and techniques depend on separating the original image into various components and then recombining them in different ways. Color images can be split into their color components (color separation — 118-19); black and white images into tonal components (tone separations — 120). Techniques include: posterization (120-121) and dye transfer (132-5).

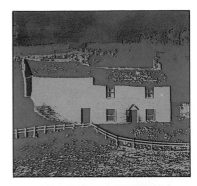

Special materials
By copying the original image onto alternative photographic materials you can create a wide range of effects. Lith film, which reduces an image to pure black and pure white and eliminates all tones of gray, is particularly useful (88-9). It can be used in all the separation techniques, and for effects such as 'neons' (130-131). Other interesting special materials include equidensity film (122-3) and dye transfer materials (132-5).

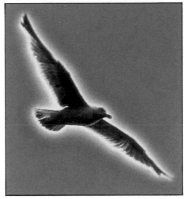

Combining images
Different photographs can be combined on the same print in an enormous number of ways. Combination techniques include: exposing the various negatives onto the same print (94-5); montaging different prints (96-101); creating mandalas (128-9); making different transfers onto the same print (82, 134-5); stripping-in (126-7).

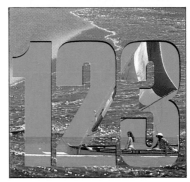

Process variations
Some of the most startling effects are created by deliberately breaking the well-established rules of the process routine. Seeming accidents can be turned into creative tools. Prints can be processed in the wrong chemicals or fogged during development to produce striking 'solarized' images (90-3).

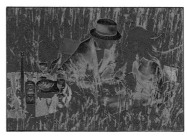

DARKROOM CHEMISTRY

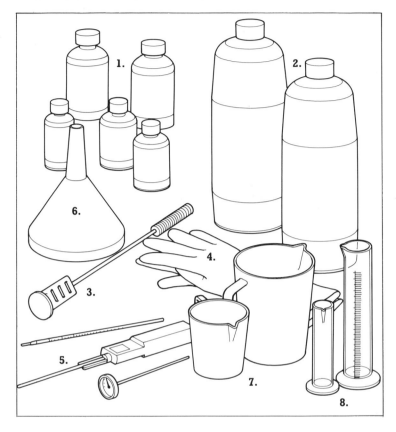

What you need

1. Glass storage bottles
2. Plastic storage bottles
3. Stirring rod
4. Rubber gloves
5. Thermometers
6. Funnel
7. Mixing jugs
8. Graduated measuring cylinders

● **Get a range of graduates** and mixing jugs, such as 1000ml, 250ml and 50ml sizes. The 1000ml is fine for measuring bulk liquids but is not sufficiently accurate for concentrated liquid developers such as Kodak HC 110.

● **Use different jugs** for each chemical if you can to prevent contamination. Otherwise, clean the jug thoroughly before you mix the next solution. Always use a different jug for bleach.

● **Never** use kitchen measures for chemicals. Not only are they insufficiently accurate, but they may also be corroded by certain chemicals and, more importantly, they may accidentally be used for mixing food afterwards.

● **Use a plastic funnel** for pouring chemicals into bottles. Make sure the funnel has an air vent to prevent blow-back from rapid filling.

● **Wear rubber gloves** when mixing toxic and corrosive chemicals such as are often found in bleaches, intensifying and reducing baths and some Cibachrome chemicals. Surgeons' gloves are better still.

● **Measure temperatures** with the right thermometer. Spirit thermometers are inexpensive and accurate enough for black and white work. For color you need a mercury thermometer.

● **Protect** a mercury thermometer by using it as a reference only. Use a cheap spirit thermometer for all your routine work, but calibrate it for accuracy against the mercury thermometer. To do this, stand both thermometers side by side in a water bath. Check the temperature on each one and write the results down — they will probably be slightly different. Now progressively add warm water, raising the temperature of the water bath half a degree at a time. Write down the reading on each thermometer at every step and plot the results on a simple graph. Use the graph to find the true reading of the spirit thermometer.

● **Never mix more solution** than you need for the job in hand. Solutions at working strength rarely last long.

● **Store chemicals** in the way recommended by the maker or in proper storage jars.

● **Keep storage jars full.** The more air there is in the jar, the shorter the life of the solutions will be. Use a concertina jar to adjust the size of the jar to suit the volume of solution, or fill the air space with marbles.

How long chemicals keep

	Working solution	Stock sol. in half-full bottles	Stock sol. in full bottles
B&W developers			
Universal developer	1 month	3 months	6 months
Fine-grain film developer	1 month	2 months	6 months
High contrast film developer (stock)	1 month	2 months	6 months
Standard paper developer*	1 day	2 months	6 months
Soft paper developer*	1 day	6 weeks	4 months
B&W Fixers and stops			
Fixer*	1 day	1 month	2 months
Stop bath*	1 day	no limit	no limit
Color film chemicals			
Negative developer	6 weeks	6 weeks	6 weeks
bleach	no limit	no limit	no limit
fixer	8 weeks	8 weeks	8 weeks
Color slide film first dev.	4 weeks	1 week	8 weeks
color dev.	8 weeks	6 weeks	12 weeks
bleach-fix	24 weeks	24 weeks	24 weeks
Color print chemicals			
Negative/positive developer	—	2 weeks	4 weeks
stop bath	—	8 weeks	8 weeks
bleach-fix	—	4 weeks	4 weeks
Positive/positive first dev.	—	1 week	2 weeks
color developer	—	1 week	4 weeks
bleach-fix	—	2 weeks	6 weeks
Cibachrome developer	—	—	4 weeks
bleach	—	—	4 months
fixer	—	—	6 months

* Keeping times for b&w paper chemicals at working strength are shown for solutions left in open processing trays.

MIXING CHEMICALS

You can still make up a few useful solutions from 'raw' chemicals, but there is little point. Commercial formulas do the job more conveniently, more efficiently, and often more cheaply too. And for many processes, only the commercial formula will give acceptable results. So for all but a few special applications, photographic chemicals are made up from convenient, easy-to-mix commercial packages. These come in the form of either liquid concentrates or in packets of powder. Liquid chemicals are very easy to use. The working solution is made simply by diluting some of the concentrate in water. Powdered chemicals are cheaper but slightly less easy to use and all the packet must be used at once. Procedures for mixing both types are outlined below.

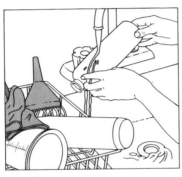

1 Wash all the containers and mixing equipment thoroughly under running water. Use ordinary household detergent to help clean stubborn stains, never anything stronger. Arrange the chemicals in the order they are to be used.

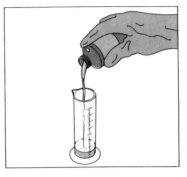

2 When mixing very concentrated liquid chemicals, such as wetting agent, start by diluting the concentrate in a small graduate. You can then add this less concentrated solution to the full quantity of water in a larger jar to give the right dilution.

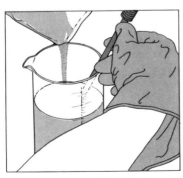

5 With powdered chemicals, add the entire contents of each packet to the water in the specified order. Stir the solution gently all the time to help dissolve the powder. Wait until each chemical is completely dissolved before adding the next packet of powder.

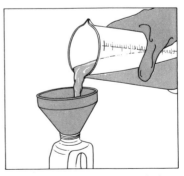

6 If you are not using the solution immediately, you can store it in a proper storage bottle. To fill the bottle, place a funnel in the neck and slowly pour in the mixed solution. Try to fill to the top to exclude air to extend the solution's life. Close the lid tightly.

● **Always add chemicals to water,** NEVER the other way round. This is especially important with chemicals containing acids.

● **Fit a filter** to the faucet if you suspect there may be tiny impurities in the water.

● **Use all the packet** with powdered chemicals. Never try to make smaller quantities of solution by using a fraction of the packet.

Some chemicals are added to the pack in a certain order so that they completely mix only when the solution is made up.

● **Clean equipment thoroughly**

● **Never use strong cleaners** such as bleach; they may contaminate the container.

● **Remove ingrained stains** with special darkroom cleaners.

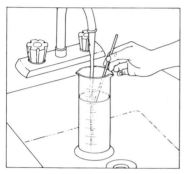

3 Measure the water into a large graduate — ideally just a little bigger than the total volume of the made-up solution. Check the temperature of the water and adjust if necessary. This is especially important with powdered chemicals.

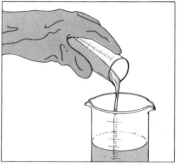

4 If you are using liquid concentrates for color chemicals and bleaches, remember to wear rubber gloves. Pour in the entire contents of the bottle or a measured amount as directed by the manufacturers into the water and stir.

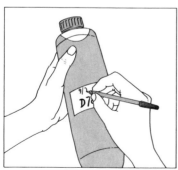

7 Label the bottle clearly, using a waterproof marker. Either write directly on the bottle or use adhesive labels. Mark the exact name of the solution, the dilution and the date of preparation. Wipe the bottle clean and store at room temperature in the dark.

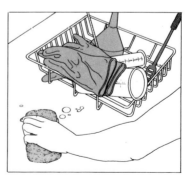

8 Wash all the mixing equipment thoroughly in water or else a proprietary darkroom cleanser. Remember to clean gloves, stirrer and thermometer as well as mixing jugs. Wipe down all the mixing surfaces immediately with a detergent-soaked sponge.

FILM PROCESSORS

If you want to process either black and white or color film, you must have a lightproof processing tank. For 35mm and roll film, you need a spiral tank. This is a cylindrical tank, made either of stainless steel or plastic, containing a reel with a spiral groove to hold the film in place. For sheet film, however, you need three deep tank processors, or a film insert for a print tube.

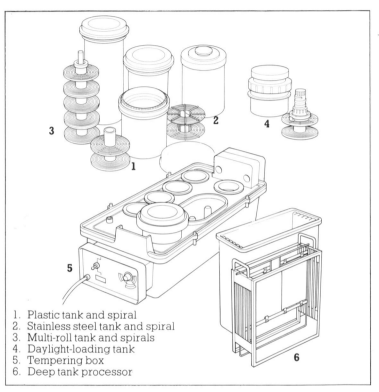

1. Plastic tank and spiral
2. Stainless steel tank and spiral
3. Multi-roll tank and spirals
4. Daylight-loading tank
5. Tempering box
6. Deep tank processor

● **Plastic or stainless steel?**
Plastic tanks are often a better bet for the beginner. They are cheap and robust, and the spiral is self-loading. But for the more experienced, a stainless steel tank may be more useful. The spiral is harder to load, but the film is less liable to stick, and the tank may be dried in an oven for rapid reuse.

● **Multi-roll tanks** can save time and money if you often have many films to process at once.

● **Daylight-loading tanks** have special spirals that allow film to be loaded in normal light. This is perfect for the photographer who processes the occasional roll. But their thirst for chemicals makes them uneconomical for regular use.

● **For regular color work,** where accurate temperature control is paramount, it may be worth buying a thermostatically-controlled 'tempering box' to keep both tank and chemicals at the right temperature.

● **Deep tank processors** are made of plastic or rubber. You need a plastic tank for processing color sheet film — color chemicals attack rubber.

PRINT PROCESSORS

All you need to process black and white prints is three open trays. You can process color prints in open trays too, but this means working in almost total darkness. For color printing, then, you need a lightproof processing tank into which all the chemicals can be poured in turn. Tanks range from the simple hand-rolled tube to sophisticated motorized, temperature-controlled processors.

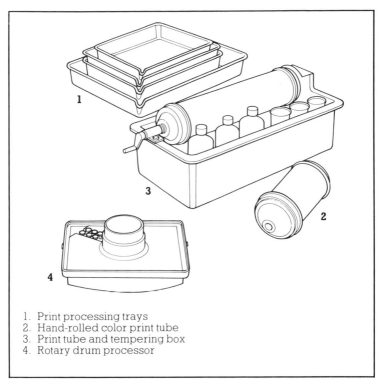

1. Print processing trays
2. Hand-rolled color print tube
3. Print tube and tempering box
4. Rotary drum processor

● **Buy three trays for b&w** print processing, a different color for each of the three solutions (developer, wash and fixer), and always use same tray for each solution.

● **Orbital processors** are usually the cheapest tanks for color printing. They are little more than curved dishes with a lid and a light-trapped hole for pouring in chemicals, but they work well and are ideal for the beginner.

● **Simple color print tubes** are agitated simply by rolling along the bench. This is fine if you have the time and patience to ensure

consistent agitation. Temperature control is slightly easier than with orbital processors.

● **A motorized tube** is a worthwhile investment if you do a great deal of color printing, saving time and ensuring print agitation is repeatable and precise.

● **Tempering boxes** take the sweat out of maintaining the accurate temperature control vital in color print processing.

THE ENLARGER

Darkroom work revolves around the enlarger, and making the right choice is crucial. Buy the best you can afford. But bear in mind that, given an equivalent lens, you can make prints on the most basic enlarger to match any made on a top-of-the-range model. An expensive enlarger is not a guarantee of high quality results. Rather, it offers a range of facilities that frees you to concentrate on making perfect prints.

● **Vertical enlargers,** in which the light is directly above the lens, make a good first buy. Their simple construction makes them noticeably cheaper than the reflex type.

● **Reflex enlargers,** in which the light is mounted horizontally and reflected through the lens from a mirror, are becoming more and more the norm — and for good reason: they are generally more compact and less prone to overheating than the traditional vertical type.

● **For black and white prints,** the best enlarger light source is a condenser. Condenser enlargers use lenses above the negative to concentrate the light, boosting contrast and cutting short exposure times.

● **For color prints,** you really need a diffuser enlarger unless you are prepared to go to great lengths to keep down dust. Hard condenser light highlights dust and scratches on the film. Diffuser enlargers have a ground glass screen to scatter and soften the light, disguising blemishes. With black and white, the gain in contrast with a condenser makes up for the effort needed to deal with dust. With color, there is no gain in contrast and a diffuser is a much better bet.

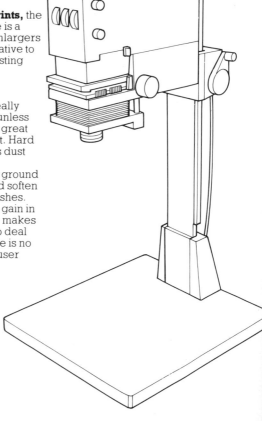

For color printing, the color of the enlarger light must be individually tailored for each picture to give correct color. This is achieved by slotting different colored filters into the light path (subtractive printing) or adjusting relative exposure times through three standard filters (additive printing). Nearly all modern enlargers have some facility for color correction ranging from a simple filter drawer to sophisticated 'dial-in' heads.

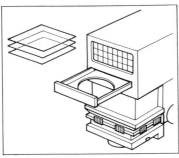

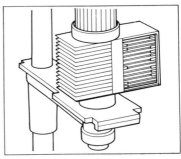

▲ The most basic system for color correction is a drawer above the negative carrier that accepts inexpensive square acetate filters. Correction is usually subtractive and yellow, magenta and cyan filters of varying density are made up into individual 'filter packs' for each picture. The system is cheap and simple and works just as well as more expensive methods. But operation is slow and tedious.

▲ One step up from the basic filter drawer is a filter panel. This is a large box set between the lamp and the negative carrier. It contains 14 filters (including a UV filter) which can be slid into the light path to give the right color balance. The system is effective and much less effort to use than the basic filter drawer, but the restricted range of filters in the panel limits its scope.

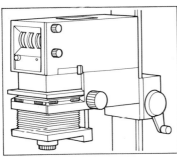

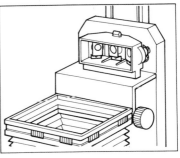

▲ Enlargers with dial-in color heads are the best for color printing, though even the cheapest cost more than a mid-range SLR camera. Dial-in heads usually have 'dichroic' filters in yellow magenta and cyan that can be dialled progressively into the light path to fine tune the color balance. Dichroic filters work by interference, not absorption, and are very resistant to fading.

▲ Enlargers based on the additive principle have three light sources (blue, green and red) and color correction is achieved by varying the brightness of each light. They are generally expensive and the system is harder to grasp than the subtractive. But they give finer control over color balance and it is much easier to create special effects such as solarization and printing b&w negatives in color.

ENLARGER MOVEMENTS

Once you have decided your price range and the type of enlarger you need, you can start to look at individual models and facilities. An important feature to look for is heavy precise construction, for one of the great shortcomings of many less expensive enlargers is vibration during exposure. A solid, well-engineered column and head is the first step on the road to quality prints.

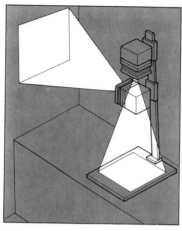

● **Look for interchangeable heads.** They not only make it easier to upgrade from black and white to color, they also mean you can use precisely the right type of head for the job without having two complete enlargers. A condenser head ideal for black and white work can be replaced in minutes with a color head complete with diffuser light and dial-in filters.

● **A tilting head** can be very useful if you often make large prints. This can often make up for a short enlarger column. By tilting the head at 90° to the column (pictured left), you can project a much bigger image on the wall than is possible on the baseboard.

● **Inclined columns** allow very large images to be projected clear of the base of the column.

● **Look for a tall column** if you plan to make many large prints. A tall column is far more convenient to use than a tilting head, but making a tall column rigid boosts the cost considerably.

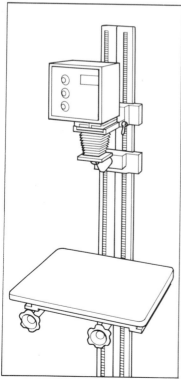

● **Double tube columns** give a much firmer support for the enlarger head. Rectangular box columns offer still firmer support.

● **Friction brakes** are cheap and simple way of locking the enlarger head on the column, but the head is harder to position accurately and not totally secure.

● **Rack and pinion systems** allow you to crank the head smoothly up and down the column precisely and securely — but they cost more.

● **A wall-mounted enlarger** (picture left) is very rigid and allows you to vary the print size accurately over a much wider range than a bench top enlarger.

ENLARGER LENSES

People often used to try to make enlargements with their camera lens, but it is now appreciated that only a lens designed specifically for the task will give high quality results. The enlarger lens is the ultimate control on the quality of your prints and it is worth getting the best you can afford. No amount of technique can make up for an inferior lens.

● **If your enlarger has a lens** fitted when you buy it, don't assume that this is the best for you. Enlarger manufacturers have to compromise to meet all kinds of demands.

● **Three-element lenses** are relatively inexpensive, but they rarely give very high resolution and are prone to vignetting — that is, darkening of the image away from the center.

● **Look for edge definition.** It is at the edge of the image, not the center that poorer quality lenses fall down.

● **Beware of vignetting** if you plan to print from slides. The high contrast of slides shows up vignetting all too distinctly. It can be reduced by stopping down, but this can mean overlong exposures.

● **Choose the focal length** to fit the format of the films you use and the size of enlargements you plan to make. Focal length is a compromise between quality and convenience. Long focal lengths give best results; short focal lengths are easier to use because they give a bigger image at a given enlarger head height. The lens must be wide enough to cover the film format without loss of quality. Look for a focal length similar to the diagonal of the film format. A 50mm lens is fine for 35mm; 6 × 6cm (2¼ in) negatives need an 80mm.

● **Don't get a lens too short** for the format. Wide angle lenses may perform well only at magnifications more suitable for a larger format.

● **Some newer wide-angle lenses** have been constructed to perform well even with small format films. They are expensive.

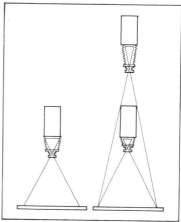

▲ Matching the focal length to the film diagonal gives the best possible results, but can mean that the enlarger head has to be raised high for large prints from small format film (right).

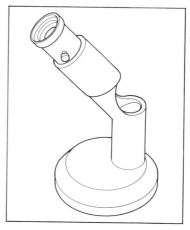

▲ Even the most expensive six-element lens will not give good results if focused badly, so it is worth buying a focus magnifier to help achieve maximum sharpness. The magnification means you focus on the film grain.

TIMERS AND METERS

Precision control is vital in many aspects of darkroom work, and there are many aids on the market to help you achieve the degree of accuracy needed. There are timers to time processes and exposures; exposure meters to determine the exposure you need for each print; and color analyzers to help you find the filtration you need for perfect color balance in a color print. None but a basic timer is absolutely essential, but each takes a little of the tedium out of darkroom work and helps maintain the consistency essential for quality results.

● **Basic universal timers,** giving times in both minutes and seconds, are quite adequate for most routine black and white work. But their limitations become clear when you start burning-in and dodging prints or trying complex color processing sequences.

● **Color processing** often involves many steps, each of different length, and a special process timer can be invaluable. Even the most basic process timer has the facility to time each stage in a long and varied sequence, up to an hour.

● **A bleep timer** is the cheapest form of exposure timer. Because it admits an audible bleep every second, it leaves your eyes free to concentrate on burning-in and dodging prints.

● **Programmable timers** are expensive but switch the enlarger on and off for you, thus ensuring completely accurate exposure timing and leaving you free to concentrate on local exposure variations.

● **Dual purpose timers** combine the functions of process and exposure timer in one unit but can cost a great deal.

● **Exposure meters** save time and money on test strips by indicating how much exposure each print will need. Meters giving an 'integrated' reading from the whole picture area are quicker to use and cheaper but less precise. With the more expensive 'spot' meters, you can take readings from chosen areas of the picture for precision exposures.

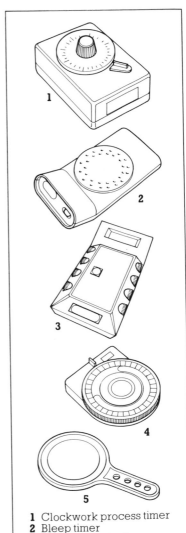

1 Clockwork process timer
2 Bleep timer
3 Programmable timer
4 Spot exposure meter
5 Spot meter diffuser

COLOR PRINTING AIDS

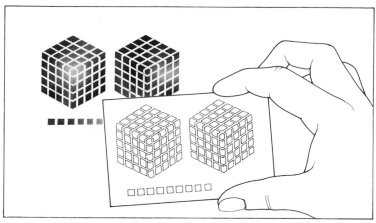

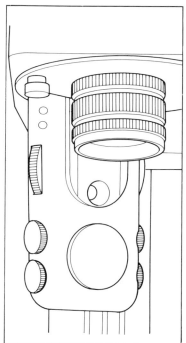

▲ Color mosaics are the cheapest and simplest form of color printing aid. With the image diffused completely, a test print is made from the negative through a mosaic of different colored filters. When the print is processed, you look for the square closest to a neutral gray to find the filtration.

▼ Color analyzing meters save you the time and expense of making test prints. Some measure the overall color of the print and 'integrate to gray' to give the correct color filtration for the negative. The more expensive meters take a 'spot' color reading, giving you all the information you need for accurate color. Both spot and integrating analyzers are expensive and you must do a great deal of color printing to justify the outlay.

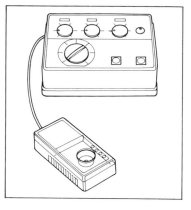

▲ Some color analyzers, like this one made by Rodenstock, have a wide range of functions. The analyzer is simply part of a color printing system that involves a set of special effects filters as well as an analyzer. The analyzer itself is attached to a special lens and a probe between the lens elements ensures an integrated color reading of the negative.

PRINT WASHERS

All prints made by conventional techniques need thorough washing after processing to remove residual chemicals. The only exceptions are systems like Agfachrome-Speed and Ektaflex which give dry prints. But the washing system you need depends on the type of paper you use. Traditional fiber-based papers absorb large quantities of chemicals and these must be soaked out slowly. Modern resin-coated (RC) papers, on the other hand, need only rapid surface washing in a stream of water to disperse the unwanted chemicals.

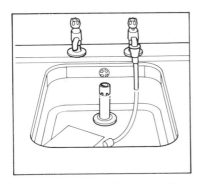

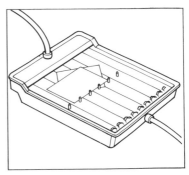

▲ The simplest and cheapest print washer is an overflow pipe that replaces the plug in an ordinary sink, allowing water to drain but keeping it at a constant level. The system is slow but fine for fiber-based prints. The drawbacks are that it prevents you using the sink for other tasks and allows you to wash only a few prints at once.

▲ High-speed washers are designed to make the most of the rapid processing qualities of RC paper, allowing water to flow rapidly over both surfaces of the print. They can wash four prints in less than three minutes, peg separators keeping prints from overlapping. You can wash fiber prints too but the flow must be very slow indeed.

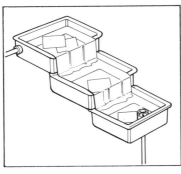

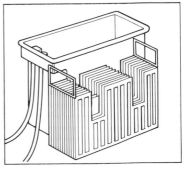

▲ To wash fiber-based prints more efficiently, you can set up a cascade washer with print trays in a bath. Clean water cascades from the top tray to the bottom, while you progressively move each print up through the trays to increasingly fresh water. Six or more prints can be washed at once.

▲ Autowashers are not cheap but are suitable for all types of paper, and take 12 large prints at once. Inflowing water rocks the cradle, ensuring thorough washing, and the compact design means that the autowasher fits neatly on the darkroom draining board, or in a sink, with room to spare.

PRINT DRYERS

You can dry prints by laying them flat on blotting paper, or by hanging them to dry, or even with the aid of a hair dryer. But if you want to dry large numbers of prints in a hurry, it is worth investing in a proper print dryer. Print dryers may also give a better finish. Unfortunately, not all dryers are suitable for both fiber-based and resin-coated papers. RC papers cannot be dried in rotary or flat-bed glazers, while fiber-based prints tend to curl in hot air dryers.

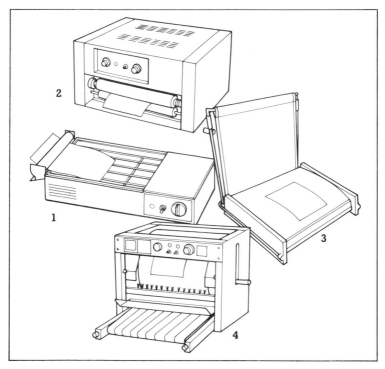

1 Manual dryer
2 Auto dryer
3 Flat-bed glazer
4 Rotary glazer

● **Manual dryers** blow hot air over the print. Temperature is controlled by a thermostat, but you have to feed the paper through the rollers by hand and take the print off the rack when it is dry.

● **Auto dryers** will take either RC or fiber-based prints straight from the washer — though fiber papers may curl. RC prints are dry in seconds and some dryers can handle 400 prints an hour. But they can cost as much as a good SLR.

● **Flat-bed glazers** give fiber-based prints a glazed or matt finish and ensure they dry without curling. The design is simple: the prints are held on a warm curved metal surface by taut canvas. So they are relatively inexpensive but they can dry less than 30 10 × 8 prints an hour.

● **Rotary glazers** can dry hundreds of fiber-based prints an hour, but they are generally too expensive for amateur use.

PREPARE TO PROCESS

If you do no other darkroom work, process your own black and white films. B&W film processing is simple, easy to master and requires the barest minimum of special equipment. You don't even need a darkroom. And only by processing films yourself can you achieve the level of consistency and control over negatives needed for high quality black and white prints.

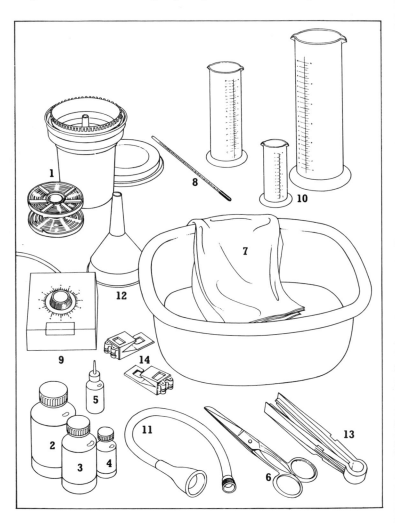

What you need

1	Film processing tank	**8**	Thermometer
2	Developer	**9**	Timer or watch with second hand
3	Stop bath	**10**	Graduates
4	Fixer	**11**	Washing tube
5	Wetting agent	**12**	Funnel
6	Scissors	**13**	Squeegee
7	Absorbent cloths	**14**	Film clips

● **A processing tank** is the one item of equipment for which there is no real substitute. To keep the cost of chemicals down, use the smallest tank you can, or save up exposed films for processing in a single batch.

● **Makeshift measures.** At a pinch, you can do without proper graduates. Liquid chemicals for b&w are mixed by proportion, not absolute volume. So when the instructions tell you to mix one part developer concentrate with, say, nine parts of water, simply add one measure — an eggcup, a whisky glass, a jamjar or whatever — to nine measures of water. But make sure the measure is never used for food or drink.

● **Use a timer** to time process steps. Although a watch with a second hand is quite accurate enough for b&w film processing, processing times are so long that it is easy to lose track of how many minutes have passed. A timer solves this problem. If you do use a watch, write down the finishing time as soon as you begin each step.

● **Beware of pointed scissors:** they can easily scratch the film as you're cutting it in the dark. Snub-nosed scissors are a much safer bet.   .

● **Use a 'universal' developer** suitable for all b&w films (and prints as well) for your first experiments in film processing. Only graduate to the more specialized developers (see page 42-43) once you can achieve completely consistent results.

● **A stop bath** between developing and fixing is not absolutely vital. Thorough rinsing in tap water is usually enough to prevent carry over of developer to the fixing stage. But a proper stop bath neutralizes the action of the developer instantly, giving much more accurate control over development time.

● **Fixer can be reused** a number of times, so remember to have a suitable brown glass bottle handy to store it.

● **Don't use detergent** as a substitute for a 'wetting agent', no matter what anyone tells you. Modern detergents are far too harsh and contain additives that leave smears on the film.

● **Warming chemicals.** To work properly, the processing solutions must be held at a constant 68°F (20°C). If you have no tempering box (see page 17), the best way to keep the solutions at the right temperature is to stand the containers in a trough of warm water until the moment they are to be used.

● **Warming the bath.** To bring the water bath to the process temperature, start with the water slightly cooler and gradually add hot water, checking the temperature all the time. This is much easier than adding cold water to bring the temperature down.

● **Label the solutions** in the order they are to be used and arrange them in order across the trough so that they fall easily to hand.

31

LOAD THE FILM

To load the film into the tank, you need complete darkness, although you can perform every other processing stage in broad daylight. A proper darkroom is by far the best place to work, but anywhere that can be made securely lightproof will do.

If you plan to process films often, but have no darkroom, think about investing in a changing bag, which is a special lightproof bag with armholes. For occasional forays, though, try loading the film in a wardrobe, in a cupboard under the stairs or even under the bedclothes. But check that it is genuinely lightproof there, remembering that it takes at least ten minutes for your eyes to adjust to the dark. To be safe, process films only at night.

Self-loading spiral

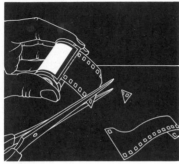

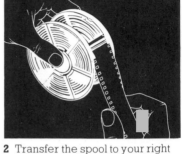

1 In complete darkness, remove the film from its cassette and cup the spool in the palm of your left hand. Using thumb and forefinger as guides, cut off the film end between perforations. Then cut off the corners to make the film easier to load.

2 Transfer the spool to your right hand. Then, with the left, hold the spiral vertically so that the lugs at the start of the spiral are at the top. Holding the spool firmly and the film end between thumb and forefinger, gently feed the film under the lugs until it catches.

Center-loading spiral

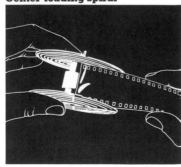

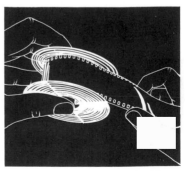

1 Stainless steel spirals are loaded from the center outwards. In darkness, open the cassette and cut off the film end, as with plastic spirals. Then, arching the film gently inwards between thumb and forefinger, guide the end towards the hub of the spiral.

2 Attach the film to the hub either by pushing it under the spring clip or hooking it on the lugs, depending which is used. Then, with your right, gently draw out a length of film (about six inches) while holding the spiral firmly in your left hand.

● **Practise loading the spiral** in daylight with an old roll of film before you risk an important film. Practise first with your eyes open, then with them shut.

● **Clean and dry the spiral** well before you load the film — any trace of moisture will make the film stick.

● **Steel spirals** can be dried by warming briefly in a low oven. DON'T try this with plastic spirals.

● **Keep a lightproof bag to hand** — a heavy duty black plastic trash bag will do. If anything goes wrong, you can chuck film, spiral and all in the bag and stop for a breather.

● **Lay out all you need** so that it falls easily to hand in the dark.

● **Open film cassettes** (in the dark) with a bottle opener if they have staples around the spool. If not, tap the end on the table.

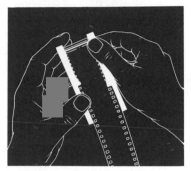

3 Once the film is slotted smoothly beneath the lugs, operate the self-load mechanism by turning the two sides of the spiral alternately to and fro. If the film sticks, wiggle it sideways a little or pull the film back out a few inches and start again. Never force the film.

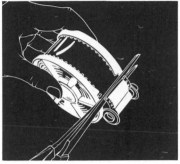

4 When all the film is in the spiral, snip off the spool and tape down the loose film end. Then drop the spiral gently into the tank, fit all the components, including locking collar and spindle, and screw or push the lid down firmly. You are now ready to start processing.

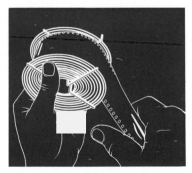

3 To take up the free length of film, turn the spiral smoothly with your left hand, keeping the film and the spiral aligned. As you turn the spiral, make sure the film is taken up. Repeat this motion until all the film is on the spiral and then cut off the spool.

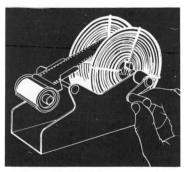

4 With a reel-loader, loading the spiral couldn't be simpler, though as with hand-loading, practice is vital. Remember not to rewind the film end right back into the cassette. With a little film protruding you can set the loader up in normal lighting.

DEVELOP AND FIX

Once the film is loaded safely into the tank, you can turn on the lights and start the processing sequence. Every darkroom worker knows just how important it is to control the process times and temperatures carefully. But I've always found that consistent technique can be just as important. The only way to achieve high quality results, and repeat them again and again, is to follow the same processing routine meticulously, right down to the last detail. If, for example, you start timing development the moment you pour developer into the tank, always do so. This way you can make minute adjustments and gradually refine your technique. Bear in mind, though, that different films require different processing routines and it helps to make a note of each change.

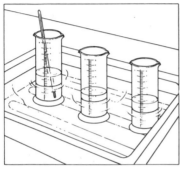

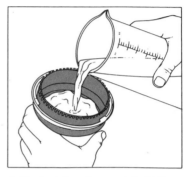

1 Before you start to develop the film, clean the thermometer thoroughly and check the temperature of the developer. If it has fallen below 68°F (20°C), add a little hot water to the water bath to raise the temperature again. Clean the thermometer after use.

2 To start development, hold the tank at 45° and pour the measured quantity of developer into the tank mouth. Pour the solution as quickly as possible, but keep the flow smooth — any air bubbles may cause uneven development. Once all the developer is in, start timing.

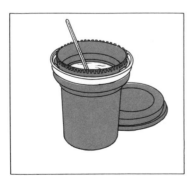

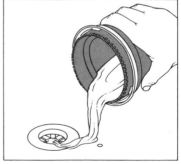

5 Towards the end of the recommended development period, check the temperature of the developer in the tank. If the temperature has dropped more than 3°F, extend the development time according to the manufacturer's instructions.

6 Start to pour the developer away ten seconds before development is completed — development will continue until you pour in the stop bath. Once the tank is empty, immediately fill the tank with stop solution, or clean water, and agitate for one minute.

● **Don't bother to pre-soak** ordinary b&w film in warm water before development. Modern developers contain wetting agents which prevent air bubbles. Chromogenic films do need pre-soaking, however.

● **Stand the tank** in the water bath for a few minutes before pouring in the developer. This should bring the tank up to the process temperature. A cold tank may upset calculations.

● **Always agitate** the same way to ensure consistent, predictable results.

● **Fix fast films slightly longer** — the emulsions often contain silver iodide which is less easily removed.

● **A milky sheen** to the film after fixing indicates exhausted fixer.

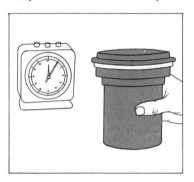

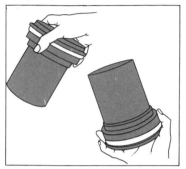

3 Immediately the tank is filled, push the lid on firmly and, with the tank upright, tap the base sharply on the bench. This should dislodge any air bubbles that may be trapped on the film. Repeat this trick every time you pour a new solution into the tank.

4 Agitate thoroughly during development. If your tank does not leak when turned upside down (test it beforehand) agitate by inverting the tank once every 20 seconds. If it leaks, agitate vigorously with the twiddle stick for five seconds every 20 seconds.

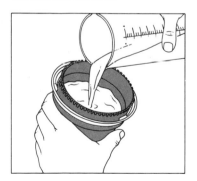

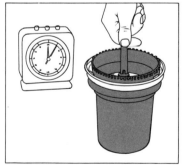

7 Pour away the stop bath and fill the tank with fixer. Remember not to use exhausted fixer, though, or the film may well be discolored. Once the tank is full, rap it sharply on the bench to dislodge air bubbles and start to agitate immediately.

8 Agitate continuously for the first 30 seconds and, thereafter, for five seconds (or two inversions) every 30 seconds. At the end of the recommended fixing period, pour the fixer through a funnel into a storage bottle for use again at a later date.

WASH AND DRY

With developing and fixing complete, it is tempting to rush through the final processing stages to see your pictures. But meticulous care is as crucial in washing and drying as any other stage. Traces of unwanted chemicals left by inadequate washing can easily stain the film or cut short the life of the negative. Careless drying can leave blemishes on the film that no amount of retouching on the print can disguise.

You can wash film in either running water or half a dozen changes of water. I usually use running water, simply because it is much less trouble. But changes of water clean the film just as well, provided you shake the tank vigorously. Recommended washing times vary, but 30 minutes is usually enough.

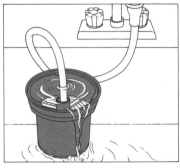 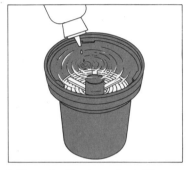

1 Stand the tank in a sink to wash the film. The best method is to direct tap water right into the bottom of the tank through a hose. If you have no hose, stand the tank open beneath the tap but empty the tank and turn over the spiral frequently.

2 Once the film is washed, fill the tank with fresh water. To ensure even drying, add a little wetting agent. For each 200ml of water, you need 10ml of wetting agent stock solution, made up by diluting a bottle of wetting agent with nine parts of water.

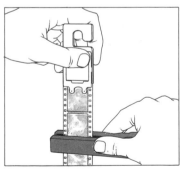 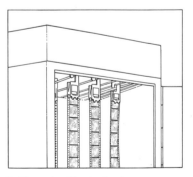

4 Gently pull on the film clip to withdraw the film from the spiral. Clean the blades of a squeegee to remove any minute grit particles. Then in a continuous stroke, run the squeegee down the film to remove all the excess water from the surface.

5 Hang the film to dry in a totally dust-free environment, preferably a proper drying cabinet. If you have problems with dust, spray the drying area with water from a garden plant spray, and keep the area fairly warm to dry the film as quickly as possible.

● **In cold winters,** wash the film in changes of water brought to 68°F in the water bath. A sudden rush of icy cold tap water can stress the emulsion, creating 'crazy paving' cracks — a fault called reticulation.

● **When you use a hardening fixer,** wash the film for twice as long.

● **Cut short washing time** when you need the film urgently by using a hypo clearing agent, followed by a brief wash in water.

● **Speed up drying** with a final rinse in ethyl alcohol diluted with ten per cent water.

● **In hard water areas,** wipe down the film especially carefully to prevent white drying marks. If the water is exceptionally hard, give a final rinse in distilled water.

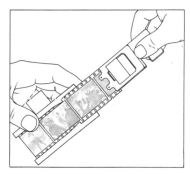

3 After the final rinse, gently shake the spiral to remove excess water. Then, with the film still in the spiral, attach a film clip to the outer end of the film. At this stage, the film is very easily damaged and the film clip makes it easier to handle safely.

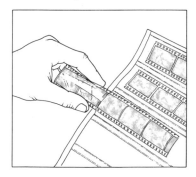

6 Once the film is dry, cut into strips six frames long. Slide the strips immediately into protective sleeves made from acid-free paper. Any delay in putting the negatives away greatly increases the chances of ending up with dusty or scratched negatives.

Process chromogenic films

Ilford's XP1 black and white film forms the image with colored dyes rather than particles of silver. This 'chromogenic' or dye-image film must be processed in a different way to conventional b&w film. Processing chromogenic b&w film is in many ways similar to color film processing (see page 68). As with color films, the fixing bath for XP1 includes chemicals that bleach away all the silver, leaving only the dye image. Similarly, for the developer to work properly, process temperatures must be high and accurately controlled.

1 Load the film into the tank.

2 Pre-soak by filling the tank with warm water at 104°F (40°C). Empty after one minute.

3 Develop for five minutes at 100°F (38°C), inverting the tank four times in the first ten seconds of each minute.

4 Bleach/fix for five minutes at 100°F (38°C), inverting the tank four times in the first ten seconds of each minute.

5 Wash in six changes of water warmed to 100°F (38°C).

6 Dry as conventional b&w film.

ASSESS THE NEGATIVE

After each film is processed and dried, take a critical look at the negatives. If there are no obvious faults, such as totally blank frames or double exposures, examine the film frame by frame through a magnifier. Minor errors in exposure and processing may be hardly noticeable at first, yet they can take that edge of quality off your prints. Unless you always make this close examination you can easily go on printing sub-standard negatives without ever appreciating why you can never achieve quite the same sparkle in your prints that the professionals manage. If you want perfect prints, strive for perfection in your negatives.

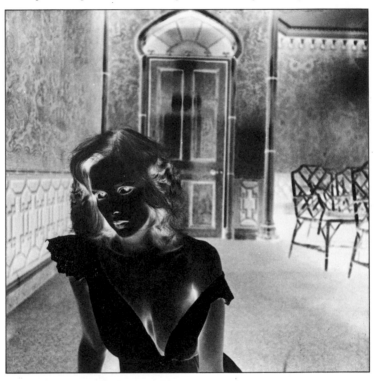

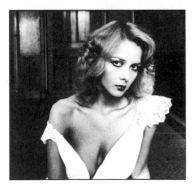

A good negative shows a full range of tones from dark to light. Detail is clearly visible in both shadows (clear areas) and highlights (dark areas). The deepest shadows in the picture are as clear as the unexposed film edges but the highlights are nowhere too dense to read type through. There is also a good range of mid-tones. Look for mid-gray edge markings on the film too. If your negatives show all these qualities, they should enlarge well and give rich prints.

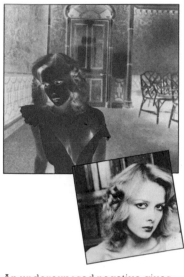

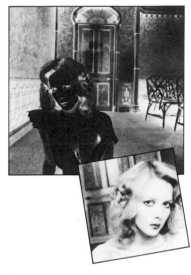

An underexposed negative gives a dark but lifeless print with poor shadow detail and contrast. The negative looks pale and thin even in the highlights while the film edge markings are normal.

An overexposed negative gives a light and flat print with poor highlight detail. The negative is dark and dense even though both the contrast range and the edge markings look normal.

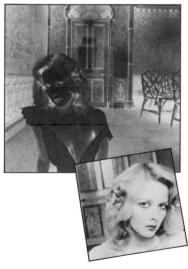

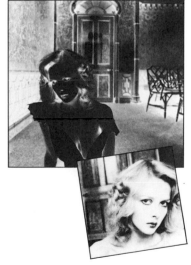

An underdeveloped negative gives a soft, low contrast print. The negative is thin and gray and the range of tones is limited. The chief symptom, though, is pale and weak edge markings on the film.

An overdeveloped negative gives an excessively contrasty print with few mid-tones. The negative has very dense highlights but fairly thin shadows. The sign here is very dark film edge markings.

EXPLOIT DEVELOPERS

Standard developers give a compromise between film speed, grain and contrast that works well for most pictures. But sometimes you need to emphasize one of these characteristics to achieve a particular effect. This is where alternative developers and processing routines come into their own.

● **Use a fine-grain developer** like Kodak D76 or Ilford ID-11 for most of your routine work. They keep visible clumping of film grains to a minimum without affecting film speed noticeably.

● **Develop films for giant prints** in an extra fine-grain developer such as Perceptol. But remember to adjust camera exposure accordingly. Perceptol cuts down film speed by one full stop.

● **Gain speed** when the film has to be underexposed by using a speed-increasing developer. Some speed-increasing developers, such as Ilford's Microphen, allow you to expose the film at two or three full stops less than the nominal film speed. Grain is increased slightly.

● **Make pictures look sharp** by using a high acutance developer. High acutance developers create an illusion of sharpness by emphasizing edges in the picture. Where a dark area meets a light area, the developer exaggerates the difference in tone, giving a dark outline to dark areas and a light outline to light areas.

● **Don't use acutance developers** with films faster than 200ISO. The increased grain size will negate the acutance effect.

● **Increase contrast** by extending development.

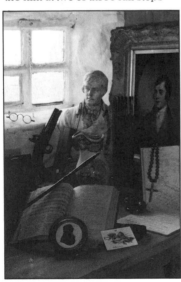

▲ Low contrast developers, like fine-grain developers, work by stopping individual silver grains from forming clumps. When used with slow films, which tend towards high contrast, fine-grain developers give negatives of normal contrast.

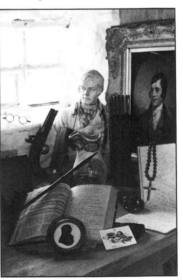

▲ General-purpose developers, either MQ or PQ, have moderate alkalinity and provide a reasonable compromise for all types of black and white materials, giving a good tonal range and fairly fine grain while retaining detail in both shadows and highlights.

Push processing
If you ever shoot in light too dim to give the shutter speed or depth of field you need with the film in your camera, try 'uprating' the film. This means exposing as if the film is faster than its nominal ISO rating. You then compensate for this underexposure by increasing the development time. This is called 'push processing'.

● **Don't push process** unless absolutely necessary. It increases grain and contrast dramatically.

● **Think in aperture stops** when uprating; it is much easier than using film speeds. Doubling the film speed simply means you can give one stop less exposure.

● **Extend development** by roughly 40% for each stop you cut exposure if in doubt. Otherwise follow directions given by the film makers. Keep standard times for chromogenic film.

● **Never push more than three stops.** Push processing not only increases grain and contrast. It also increases 'development fog'. The gain in contrast initially offsets this, but beyond three stops the fog overwhelms all shadow detail.

● **Use a speed-increasing developer** such as Microphen. This will boost shadow development at the expense of highlights, so compensating for the gain in contrast when pushing.

● **Use a two-bath developer** to gain big increases in film speed. The first component develops highlights but is quickly exhausted. The second then develops the shadows.

● **Try clip tests** with important films. This means clipping the end off the films and processing at various times to find the time that gives best results with each roll of exposed film.

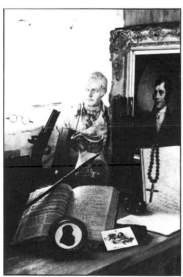

▲ High-contrast developers are very highly alkaline. They produce negatives with dense highlights and thin shadows. This degree of contrast is not usually needed in normal negatives and HC developers are usually meant only for line and lith film.

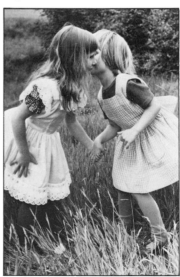

▲ High-acutance developers give an illusion of sharpness and help retain detail by concentrating development near the surface of the emulsion and by increasing edge contrast in the negative. They work best with films slower than ISO 200.

PREPARE TO PRINT

The print is the culmination of the long process that begins when you first frame the subject in the viewfinder, and it is worth taking great pains to achieve the finest quality you can. Remember, people judge the photograph by the print, as well as the original idea. No-one will appreciate the subtle gradations of light if the print is muddy and flat. To get an idea of the quality possible, try to see the work of master printers like Ansel Adams, not in reproduction but as photographic prints. Adams regards the print as a vital part of the creation of a photograph: if 'the negative is the score . . . the print is the performance.'

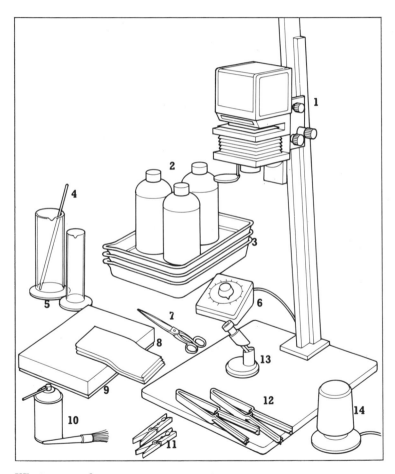

What you need
1. Enlarger
2. Developer, fixer and stop
3. Three processing trays
4. Spirit thermometer
5. Graduates, one large, one small
6. Exposure timer
7. Scissors
8. Absorbent cloths
9. Print paper
10. Dust removers
11. Clothes pegs
12. Print squeegees
13. Magnifying focus finder
14. Safelight

Making a print
1 Make a contact sheet
2 Choose the negative
3 Compose the image
4 Select the paper
5 Set up the enlarger
6 Test for exposure
7 Expose the print
8 Process the print

● **The darkroom** need only be big enough to contain the enlarger and a surface for three processing trays. If need be, you can carry the print to the kitchen for washing. If you do wash prints outside the darkroom, though, remember not to open the darkroom door while unfixed paper is lying on the bench, and use a spare tray to carry the dripping print.

● **Match safelight and print paper** for maximum light in the darkroom. Most print papers can be safely handled in a fairly bright amber light such as Kodak's safelight OC. The traditional, much dimmer red light is only needed for working with lith film. Some variable contrast papers may be fogged by the OC, however, so check the maker's recommendations.

● **Cheap acrylic safelights** are not always totally safe. Check their safeness as below and leave paper exposed for the minimum time.

● **Check your safelight** by exposing paper under the enlarger with an exposure long enough to give a light gray print. But before processing the print, leave a coin on the exposed paper for two minutes under the safelight. If the outline of the coin is visible after processing, the safelight is not safe.

● **Garden seed trays** and cat litter trays are cheap alternatives to proper photographic trays, but they are harder to use because they are shallower and less rigid.

● **Keep the darkroom at 68°F** (20°C) as nearly as you can. This is the best way to maintain the chemicals in the open trays at the right temperature.

Dealing with dust
● **Beware of dust** when printing: it ruins more prints than virtually any other single fault. Keep the darkroom as clean as possible at all times.

● **Clean with a vacuum cleaner** rather than a brush or duster. A brush will simply lift dust into the air, not remove it.

● **Wipe up chemical spillages** at once. If they are allowed to dry out they can add to the dust in the air.

● **Mix chemicals outside** the darkroom, especially if working with powders.

● **Wipe surfaces regularly** with a damp cloth.

● **Don't use a fan heater** to keep the room warm; a bar heater is much less dusty.

● **Clean each negative** carefully before printing with an anti-static blower brush.

● **Put the negative away** as soon as you finish printing.

● **Use a glassless negative carrier** in the enlarger, or at least one with a single glass, when printing from 35mm or smaller negatives. Glass surfaces attract dust and in a double glass carrier there are four surfaces for dust to settle. But if you use a glassless carrier, keep exposures brief or the negative will curl.

PROCESS THE PRINT

One of the attractions of b&w printing is that you can watch the print all the way through the processing sequence. In particular, you can assess the image as it appears in the developing bath and control development accordingly. Modern high-speed developers in combination with resin-coated (RC) papers have cut developing times so much that the chances for manipulation are considerably less than they used to be. But you may still be able to rescue a slightly overexposed print, for instance, by cutting short development. Or boost contrast by underexposing the print and extending development. Before you try to experiment with alternative processing routines, though, be sure you can achieve consistent results with the standard routine.

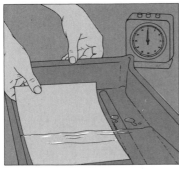

1 Prepare for processing by filling the trays with developer, stop and fixer to a depth of about ¾in (2cm). To start processing, raise one end of the developing tray about 1½in (4cm), then quickly slide the exposed print, face up, into the shallow end.

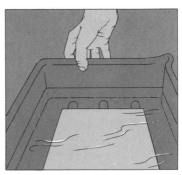

2 Immediately lower the tray so that a wave of developer completely covers the print. Start timing development. With a high-speed developer, the image should start to appear after about six seconds. Move the print around constantly.

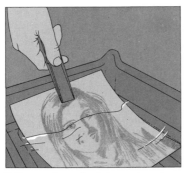

5 Lower the print face up into the fixer and agitate by rocking the tray gently for the first 15-20 seconds. Be sure all the print is continuously covered in fixer. After one minute (five for fiber-based prints), it is safe to switch on normal white light.

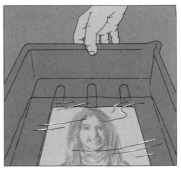

6 Rock the tray occasionally until the recommended fixing time is up. With RC papers, fixing time can be two minutes or even less with combinations such as Ilfospeed paper and Hypam fixer. Fiber-based papers must usually be fixed for ten minutes.

● **Stick to makers' process times** unless you have a very good reason for variation. Only the recommended process times will give optimum results.

● **If you vary development** by eye, remember that prints look darker and more contrasty by safelight than normal daylight.

● **Keep solutions at 68°F (20°C)** as near as possible, by standing the tray in warm water or, better, on a thermostatically-controlled tray warmer. There is some margin for error with b&w print processing — processing simply speeds up if the developer is too hot (up to a point), and slows down if it is too cold. But only by keeping temperatures near 68°F can you ensure consistent results.

● **Speed up drying** by blowing the print with a hair dryer.

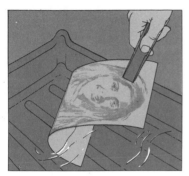

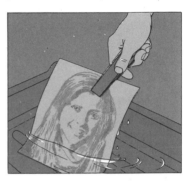

3 As soon as the image begins to appear, turn the print over and leave face down until the last third of development time. Then, turn it face up and continue agitating. When development is complete lift the print and allow developer to drain away for a few seconds.

4 Once development is complete, lower the print into the stop bath. With RC papers, this bath can be water; with traditional fiber-based papers you need an acid stop bath. Rock the tray of stop bath for about half a minute, then lift the print and let it drain briefly.

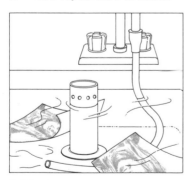

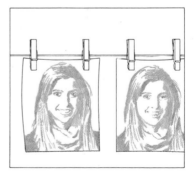

7 Wash the print in running water for four minutes (30 minutes for fiber-based papers). But be careful that prints do not stick together in the basin. Keep the water between 70 and 75°F (20-25°C) or use five changes of warm water instead.

8 Wipe excess water from the surface of the print with a print squeegee in a single continuous stroke. Then dry the print either by hanging it up or laying flat on a sheet of newspaper or in a drying rack. Fiber-based papers take much longer to dry than RC.

MAKE A CONTACT PROOF

To help decide which negatives to print, I always make a contact proof from every film. A contact proof is simply a positive print of all the frames on the film, made by exposing the whole film in contact with a single sheet of print paper. It provides not only a wealth of information to guide you when you make an enlargement, but also an easy-to-file source of reference for every one of your pictures. Cut into strips of six frames, a full 36-exposure roll of 35mm film fits neatly on to a 10×8in sheet.

Contact proofs are easy to make. All you need besides a darkroom and print processing materials are a controllable light source to expose the print — the enlarger is ideal — and a sheet of glass to hold the negatives firmly against the print paper.

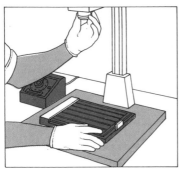

1 Before making your first contact proof, you must work out the exposure needed. To do this, place the contact frame or glass on the enlarger baseboard. Switch on the enlarger light and move the head until the light fully covers the frame. Stop the lens down to $f11$.

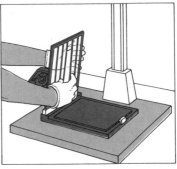

2 To make the test, place a strip of clear film from a film end under the center of the glass. Switch on the safelight and turn off the room and enlarger light. Take a sheet of print paper from its packet and cut off a small strip. Place the rest of the sheet in the packet and reseal.

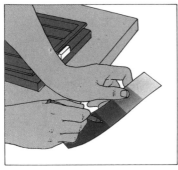

5 Once the test strip is ready, examine it in normal room lighting. The strip should have a series of gray bands. Find the first band that gives a full black (next to a dark gray band) and work out how long this band was exposed for. This is the proof exposure.

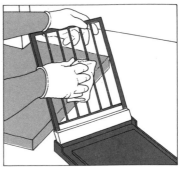

6 Clean both sides of the glass very carefully using a blower brush and an antistatic cloth. Take the negatives you wish to proof from their storage sleeves. Gently clean off fingerprints and drying marks from the shiny side of the film with a soft, lint-free cloth.

● **Use a proper contact frame** if you make many proofs. They align the negatives neatly and print markings for film information.

● **Mark the height** of the enlarger head on the column when you make your test exposure, or measure the height of the head and write it down. You can then set the head at the same height again and use the exposure established by your test for all subsequent proofs from the same film type.

● **Use grade 2 paper** to give a good indication of the tonal range you can expect in enlargements.

● **If you have no enlarger,** try exposing with a desk lamp held at various heights above the print.

● **If every test band is black,** you have exposed too much. Repeat the test with shorter exposures.

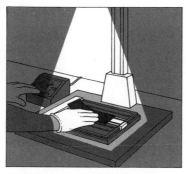

3 Place the strip of paper right under the clear film. Cover all but a fifth of the strip with a sheet of opaque card. Then switch on the enlarger light and start timing at once. After five seconds have elapsed, move the card to uncover a further fifth of the strip.

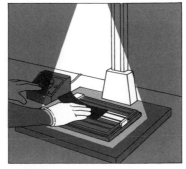

4 Continue to uncover successive fifths of the strip every five seconds, until the entire strip has been exposed. Switch off the enlarger and remove the strip of paper from under the glass. Still under safelight, process, wash and dry the print normally.

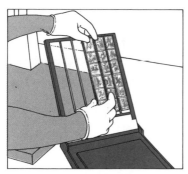

7 Carefully slide the negatives into the tracks on the frame, handling only the film edges. Keep the shiny side of the film up against the glass. If you are using a plain sheet of glass, lay the negatives on print paper under safelight.

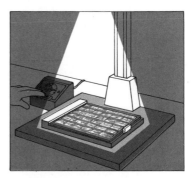

8 Under safelight again, take out a full sheet of print paper and lay it, shiny side up, in the contact frame. Lock the glass cover in place. Switch on the enlarger to make the tested exposure. Process normally. With plain glass, lay the glass over paper and negatives.

USE THE CONTACT PROOF

A good contact proof shows at a glance which images are not worth printing up. But close inspection through a magnifying lupe can actually reveal much more. You can see if images are critically sharp; if detail is present in both highlights and shadows; if pictures suffer from unwanted distractions; and so on. You can also see clearly which pictures work and which don't, and if any can be improved by close cropping.

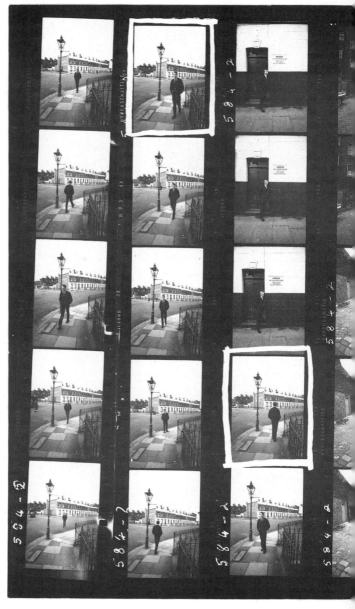

- **Make a contact proof**
work. Use it to gain all the
information you need to make the
best print from each negative.

- **Use an old slide mount** to view
each frame, undistracted by the
surrounding frames.

- **Mark-up the contact proof** with
wax or 'chinagraph' pencils so that
the markings can be wiped off.
Ring the images you wish to use.

- **Decide how to crop** each frame
with a pair of opposing L-shaped
cards. Mark the crop on the proof.

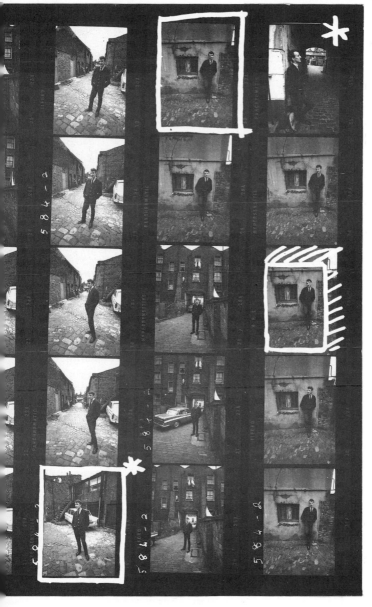

CHOOSE THE PAPER GRADE

To make the most of your pictures, you need to match carefully each negative and the paper you print on. Print paper comes in a range of different contrast grades, usually numbered from 0 to 5, but, ideally, you would print all your negatives on Grade 2 or 3 paper, except when you want a special effect. Grades 2 and 3 give a print with a good range of tones from a perfectly exposed, perfectly developed negative with an average range of densities. On Grade 4 or 5 paper, such a negative gives a hard, contrasty print with a lack of mid tones; on Grade 0 or 1, the print is soft and flat. However, because many negatives are inevitably imperfectly exposed or developed, and many subjects do not have an average range of densities you must often use the more extreme paper grades to get good prints.

In choosing paper grades, I usually aim to achieve a range of tones matching that in a print from an average negative on Grade 2 or 3 paper. So I print a soft, flat negative on hard Grade 4 or 5 paper, and a hard contrasty negative on soft Grade 0 or 1 paper.

● **Standardize on one grade** of paper and try to make all your negatives match this paper. Grade 2 is an ideal standard grade.

● **Different brands of paper** may give different contrast characteristics for the same paper grade.

● **Change brands** to find 'half grades' in between the grades of one brand.

● **Use a soft grade of paper** for contact proofs and work prints for important prints. Only a soft print will reveal textures and tonal differences in all the negative.

● **Print one grade harder** than ideal then burn-in and dodge missing details and tones. This will give a punchier print than the correct grade.

● **Print underdeveloped negatives** on hard Grade 4 or 5 paper to maximize contrast.

● **Print overdeveloped negatives** on soft Grade 0 or 1 paper to bring out the mid tones correctly.

● **Variable contrast papers** save you buying paper in a range of different grades. Variable contrast papers, such as Kodak Polycontrast and Ilford Multigrade II, have two emulsions, one high contrast and one low.

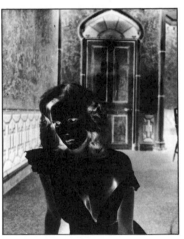

▲ Prints on various grades of paper from the negative above. The negative is well exposed and developed and has a good range of tones. Printed on Grade 0 or Grade 1 paper, the full range of tones and detail is retained. But there are few deep blacks and few bright highlights — even the girl's white dress is slightly gray. The overall effect is muddy and flat. The negative prints well on both Grade 2 and 3 paper, but the softer Grade 2 print is better because the scene is fairly contrasty. On Grade 4 paper, shadows are deep and highlights poor but detail is disappearing. On Grade 5, mid tones and shadow and highlight detail are lost almost completely.

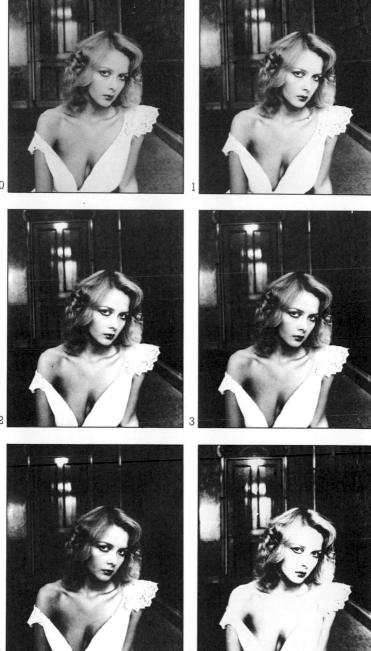

0

1

2

3

4

5

51

PREPARE TO ENLARGE

When making prints, careful preparation of the enlarger is surprisingly important. Slight errors in focusing, small specks of dust on the negative and inaccurate cropping can all take the edge off otherwise good prints. Dust on the negative is a particularly common problem. Remember, a small speck of dust will be enlarged on the print as much as the negative itself. Extra care in setting up the enlarger will be well rewarded in the final print.

In choosing what size to make your enlargement, don't be tempted to try unreasonably large prints. Big prints certainly have extra visual impact, but they are expensive to make and magnify all deficiencies. To make giant prints from 35mm negatives, you need quality equipment and superb technique.

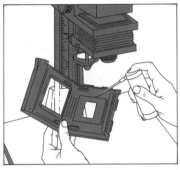

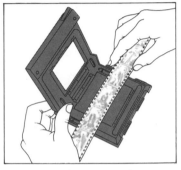

1 To prepare to enlarge, first clean the lens carefully with a soft brush and tissue. Then remove the negative carrier and dust it with a blower brush or a jet of compressed air. With glass negative carriers, carefully wipe off any fingermarks.

2 Hold the chosen negative obliquely in the enlarger beam to check for dust spots. Flick dust off with a soft brush; if any dust clings to the film, try using an antistatic pistol. Then lay the negative in the carrier so that all the frame you wish to print is visible.

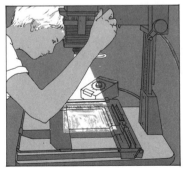

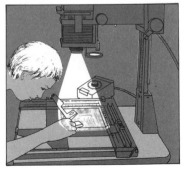

5 Adjust the focus control on the enlarger head until the image on the easel appears perfectly sharp. As you adjust the focus, the image size may change a little. If so, gradually raise or lower the enlarger head until the image is the correct size once more.

6 Now fine tune the focus, preferably with a focus magnifier. With a focus magnifier you must have a sheet of print paper on the easel to ensure the image is in the right plane. Use the grain pattern to focus. Chromogenic film has no grain, so focus on fine detail.

● **Be prepared to crop 35mm images,** or accept a little wasted paper. Surprisingly, there is no standard paper size to match the 35mm format.

● **Consider perspective.**
Theoretically, correct perspective is achieved only when the print size and viewing distance correspond with the focal length of the picture-taking lens. Thus, with the standard 50mm lens for 35mm, only a 5 × 8in (12 × 18cm) print gives correct perspective when viewed from 10in (25cm). It is worth bearing in mind that, except for special effect, prints of shots with long lenses should be smaller, or viewed from further away, than prints of wide angle shots. Similarly, prints to be mounted in a confined space, such as a hall, should be smaller than prints to be displayed in a large room.

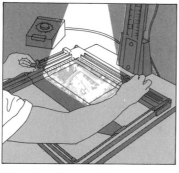

3 Replace the negative carrier in the enlarger and check that it is properly in position. Adjust the masks on the easel until they give the print size you have chosen. Center the frame under the enlarger, turn off the room lights and switch on the enlarger.

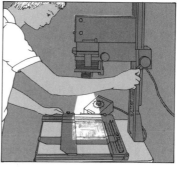

4 Open the enlarger lens to its maximum aperture to give the brightest possible image. Focus the image roughly, then slowly raise or lower the enlarger head — usually by turning the crank on the column — until the image exactly fits the frame on the easel.

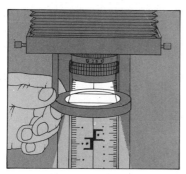

7 Once the image is perfectly sharp, remove the sheet of paper from the easel, being careful not to jog it at all. Then very gently swing the red filter across beneath the lens; any violent movement may completely upset the focus of the enlarger.

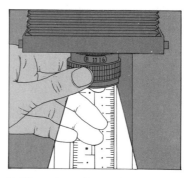

8 Close the enlarger lens down at least two stops below its maximum aperture to ensure the image is as sharp as possible. As you change the aperture, the focus may shift slightly on some enlargers. If so, quickly run through the focusing procedure again.

TEST FOR EXPOSURE

Once the enlarger is set up and focused, you need to work out just what exposure the negative requires. An experienced printer can often guess the exposure from the brightness of the image on the baseboard and then adjust for any error by watching the print in the developer. The less experienced must rely on test strips and exposure meters.

Test strips seem tedious and use a great deal of expensive paper, but they are really the only completely reliable way of establishing exposure. The correct exposure is the exposure you want; a meter can only give an average exposure. Only a test strip arms you with the information you need to give the exposure needed to give the best print from each negative.

● **Make large test strips.** Small strips are a false economy. To give an accurate indication of the exposure, each band must include enough variation of tone to be representative of the whole print.

● **Lay the strip diagonally** across the picture. In landscapes this ensures that the strip includes both sky and land.

● **Stop down the aperture** one more setting if exposures shorter than five seconds give over-exposed results.

● **Use the same exposure** as indicated by the test strip for all similar prints from the same roll of film.

● **Calibrate an exposure meter** by printing a typical negative to give the density you want in your prints. Store the exposure time given for this print in the meter's memory and it will give prints of similar density for all that batch of paper.

● **Calibrate a spot meter** more carefully than an integrating meter.

● **Use a spot meter** to select the paper grade by comparing the densities of the shadows and highlights.

● **Convert a spot meter** to an integrating meter for quickfire prints by holding a sheet of frosted acetate under the enlarger to diffuse the image.

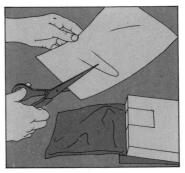

1 Under safelight, take a sheet of paper from the packet. Then with a sharp pair of scissors, cut a long broad strip from the sheet. The strip should be at least two inches wide, even with 10×8in paper. Put the rest of the sheet safely back in the packet and close the box.

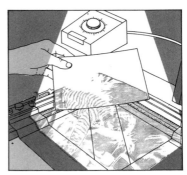

4 After five seconds, switch off the enlarger. Stop the timer and cover a fifth of the test strip with opaque card, being careful not to move the test strip in the slightest. When the card is in position, switch on the enlarger and start timing again.

● **Simplify exposure tests** by using a proprietary step-wedge. A step-wedge is a sheet of film with windows of varying densities. These densities correspond to various exposure times. To use a step-wedge, you simply lay it over the printing paper and make an exposure. Because of the different film densities, different parts of the print will get different exposure.

● **Expose a wedge for 60 seconds,** unless otherwise specified. The number by the window that gives correct exposure will give the print exposure in seconds.

● **Reduce the exposure** for the step-wedge to fine tune exposure. Then adjust the times marked by the windows correspondingly.

● **Don't use a step wedge** for difficult or large prints.

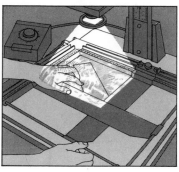

2 Check that the red filter still covers the lens and switch on the enlarger. Lay the strip of paper on the image so that it shows both dark and light tones. Place a large sheet of opaque card nearby. Turn off the enlarger and swing back the red filter.

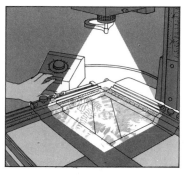

3 Wait until all the vibrations from moving the red filter have died down. Then switch on the enlarger and start timing. Get opaque card ready to slide into position for the next stage of the exposure. Keep your eye on the timer all the time.

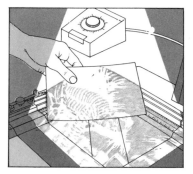

5 After a further ten seconds, switch off the enlarger and cover a further fifth of the strip. Switch on the enlarger and start timing again. Repeat this procedure after 20 and 40 seconds, covering a further fifth of the card each time, until the whole card is covered.

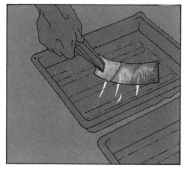

6 Develop the print for the recommended time, rinse, fix and leave to try. When the strip is dry, examine it closely in normal daylight. Work out the exposure time for the best band in the strip. This is your main print exposure, or the base for further tests.

MAKE A PRINT

With the paper chosen and an exposure established, you can make the first full print from the negative. For most photographers, this first full print is also the final print. For many master printers, however, it is only a beginning, one of a series of work prints that provide all the information needed to create a fine print. Few people can afford to adopt this approach all the time, and the first print should be quite adequate for handing round to family and friends. But if you are producing a print for mounting or for a show, it is worth making a whole series of work prints, gradually refining the balance of tones at each step. Aim to achieve good deep blacks and brilliant whites at the first step. Then go on to fill in all the subtle mid tones.

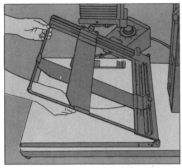 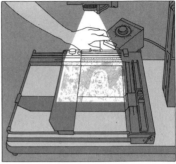

1 To make a print, pull a full sheet of paper from the packet under safelight. Lift up the easel masks and slide the paper against the stops. Gently lower the easel masks onto the paper.

2 Put your hand under the lens to block off the light and turn on the enlarger. Wait for ten seconds or so for the vibrations to die down. Swing your hand clear to start the exposure. Start timing at once.

Improve blacks
Many amateur prints lack punch because the blacks are weak. To ensure full blacks:

● **Use glossy paper,** unless the print is to be displayed under highly directional lighting.

● **Always match developer and paper.**

● **Always develop fully.** If you cut short development, some exposed grains may not be converted to black silver.

● **Never underexpose,** even if you overdevelop to increase contrast. To make the most of the paper's capacity it must be fully exposed.

● **Test the maximum black** that a paper can give by fogging a sheet completely and developing for twice the recommended time.

● **Beware of vibration** during the exposure. It can blur a print just as badly as camera shake can blur a negative.

● **Use an exposure timer,** if you have one, to start and end the exposure: it will minimize vibration.

● **Don't touch the enlarger** during the exposure. Take particular care when dodging or burning-in.

● **Print at night** when traffic is light if vibrations from passing lorries or trains are a problem.

● **Don't walk about** during the exposure — loose floorboards may shake the enlarger.

● **If light spills** from the lamphouse of your enlarger, it may fog the print. Paint the wall behind matt black to cut down reflections.

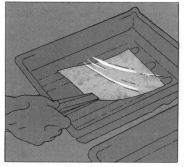

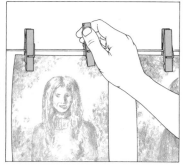

3 At the end of the tested exposure time, switch off the enlarger. Draw the paper from the easel and transfer to the developer. Develop the print for the recommended time.

4 After rinsing in a stop bath, fix the print for three minutes. Then transfer to fresh fixer and fix for a further three minutes, agitating continuously. Wash and dry the print normally.

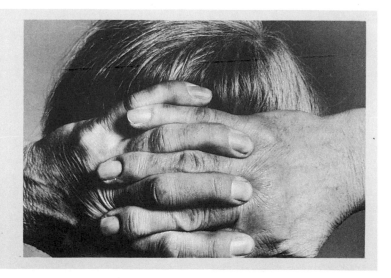

BURN IN HIGHLIGHTS

With some negatives, contrast is so extreme that you cannot get good detail in the highlights, even on the softest grade of paper, without badly overexposing the shadows. Printing on soft paper may rob the picture of all its impact anyway, as mid tones and shadows merge indistinguishably. The solution is to use the grade of paper that is correct for all but the highlights and then 'burn in' the highlights. This is done simply by giving the whole print the correct exposure, then masking all but the highlights while a further exposure is made.

● **Burn in the sky** in landscape pictures. The contrast between sky and land is often so great that all the sky is pale and uninteresting in a straight print. By burning in the sky, you can restore cloud detail and give the sky a little tone and drama. Be careful not to overdo it.

● **Use your hands for masking** as much as possible. Using hands gives you a much better 'feel' for the technique and encourages you to make subtle improvements which you might ignore if you were working with cut-out masks.

● **Use a footswitch** to control the enlarger to leave your hands free for print exposure control.

● **Stop down the lens** to give a long enough exposure for you to burn-in in a controlled way.

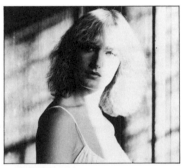

◀ In a straight print, the highlights, such as girl's hair, are almost pure white. To flesh out the highlights, I cut out a card mask for the entire print, leaving a hole for the highlight areas. First I exposed the whole print for 20 seconds. Then I held the mask over the paper to burn in the highlights for a further 12 seconds to give the print above. While burning-in, I moved the mask continuously to prevent a hard edge line appearing in the print.

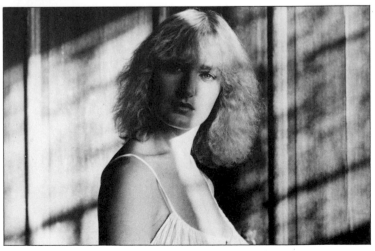

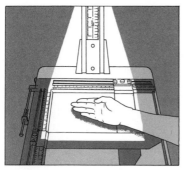

▲ You can shade the print during exposure to burn in highlights by moving your hand continuously over all the print with the exception of the highlights.

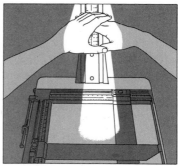

▲ Keep your hand close to the print. Burn in the central area of a print by making a ring with your hands and holding them just beneath the lens.

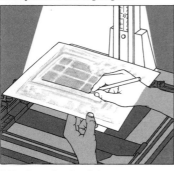

▲ For burning in elaborate highlight shapes, it is worth making a card mask. To make the mask, place a piece of card under the enlarger and mark out the highlight areas. Cut these from the card with a scalpel.

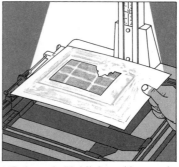

▲ To burn in highlights with a card mask, make the normal print exposure. Switch off the enlarger and move the card into place. Switch on the enlarger again. Keep the mask moving a little to prevent it showing on the print as a hard edge.

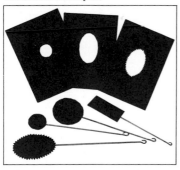

▲ You can make a variety of all-purpose masks for both burning-in and dodging (see page 60). Dodging masks must generally be held on the end of a thin rigid wire.

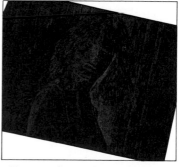

▲ To exert fine control over tones in the picture you can make masks of tissue paper. By varying the number of layers of tissue, you can control the exposure precisely.

DODGE IN SHADOWS

Just as some prints are improved by burning in the highlights, so you can 'dodge' shadows to ensure detail and tone is retained. Dodging, like burning-in, involves using masks to control the exposure received by different areas of the print. The difference is that dodging entails holding back the exposure in the shadows while giving the rest of the print the normal exposure.

● **Establish local exposure** with the aid of test strips.

● **Pivot the wire handle** around the mask when dodging near the center of the print — otherwise the white shadow of the wire may appear in the print.

● **Keep masks moving** while dodging and burning-in to soften the edges of the masked area so that it merges with the print.

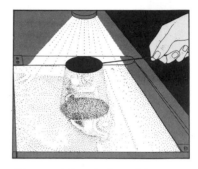

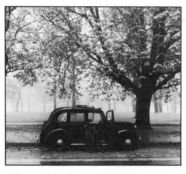

◀ In a straight print from this negative, the London taxi driver is lost in the shadow of his cab. To stop the cab and driver going so dark, I decided to dodge the print. The exposure for the straight print was 20 seconds. So I exposed the whole print for 10 seconds and then held a simple circular dodging mask over the cab for the remaining 10 seconds exposure. The result was that the cab driver was rendered lighter and became clearly visible against the dark of the cab.

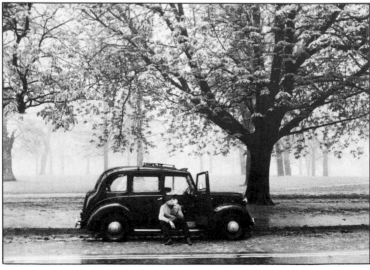

CONTROL LOCAL CONTRAST

With variable contrast paper, you can not only control exposure locally, you can also control contrast. If the contrast in one area of the print needs boosting or cutting back to create the best effect, you can use masks in the same way as burning-in and dodging exposure. The contrast rating of variable contrast paper varies according to the color of the filter it is printed through. So by printing some areas of the print through one color filter and others through another color, you can achieve the contrast you want in each part of the picture. An important point to bear in mind if you try this technique is that the exposure needed varies with contrast grade used. Remember this when you calculate the exposure needed for each part of the picture.

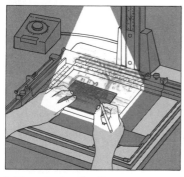

1 To make local adjustments to contrast with variable contrast paper, cut a mask from card to match the desired area. If you wish to boost tone separation in a shadow area, say, while retaining normal contrast elsewhere, cut a mask for the shadow area.

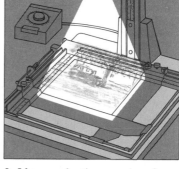

2 After conducting a series of tests to establish the relative exposure needed, expose the entire print through the filter grade right for the area to be masked. For increased shadow contrast, expose through the filter that gives the hardest grade (no. 7).

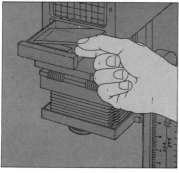

3 After the correct exposure time for the area to be masked, switch off the enlarger. Carefully insert the filter that gives the right contrast for the remainder of the print. If the shadows are to be masked, a filter that gives a softer grade (no. 4, say) is appropriate.

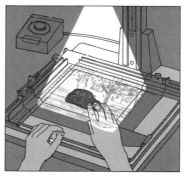

4 Holding the mask in place over the print, make the second part of the exposure. Usually, this part will be shorter since its purpose is mainly to fill in details and tone. Keep the edge of the mask moving during exposure to prevent it registering on the print.

VIGNETTE THE IMAGE

To give your pictures an old-fashioned look or to focus attention on the center of the image, you can 'vignette' the print. In a vignetted print, the subject fades gradually into a black or white surround, an effect particularly attractive with portraits. A vignette is achieved, like burning-in and dodging, by masking the needed print area, but feathering the edges during exposure. A normal vignette brings the subject forward; a reversed vignette (with a black surround) creates an impression of depth.

▼ Prints vignetted against a dark surround tend to be moody and dramatic and the effect is enhanced by similarly low key lighting. The dark vignette below was made by first exposing normally for the whole print. Then the negative was removed from the enlarger and an oval mask was held just beneath the lens to mask the boy. The rest of the print was then thoroughly fogged by switching on the enlarger for three minutes with the aperture at the widest setting.

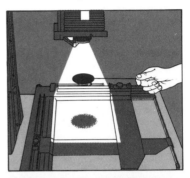

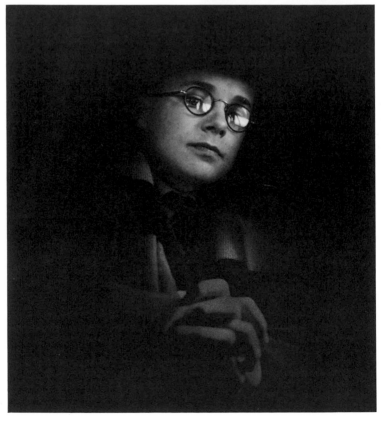

▼ Prints vignetted against a light surround are lighter in feel and work better if the lighting in the shot is pale and high key. This is especially true if you are trying to get a period feel — perhaps because we expect old prints to have faded. To create a white vignette, cut out a mask with an oval hole in the center. Then holding this mask roughly halfway between the lens and the easel, make a normal exposure for the center of the image. The picture below was then underdeveloped.

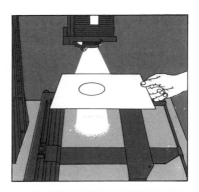

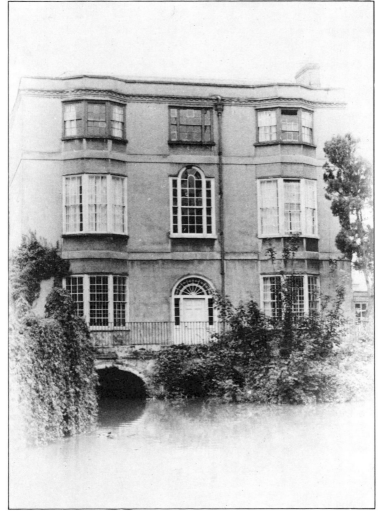

CONTROL PERSPECTIVE

If you point your camera upwards to include the top of a tall building in the frame, you will inevitably find that all the vertical lines in the picture seem to converge unnaturally. This is in fact true perspective, but in a picture it looks very odd. Fortunately, you can align all but the most sharply converging verticals during printing by deliberately tilting the printing easel to distort the print and then cropping to restore the shape.

● **Compose and focus** the image on the enlarger easel as usual.

● **Tilt the easel upwards** at the bottom end of the picture, so that it is nearer the enlarger lens. Note how the perspective straightens out.

● **Prop the easel** in place when the perspective is natural.

● **Crop the picture** where it widens at the top, farther away from the lens, by moving the easel masks inwards.

● **Stop down the lens** to maximize depth of focus and keep all the print sharp.

● **Shade the print** progressively from top to bottom during exposure because the bottom is farther from the lens and needs more exposure.

▼ To frame the dome neatly in the archway while leaving a good clean area of sky between, I had to get very close to the foreground. Being so close meant that converging verticals were inevitable.

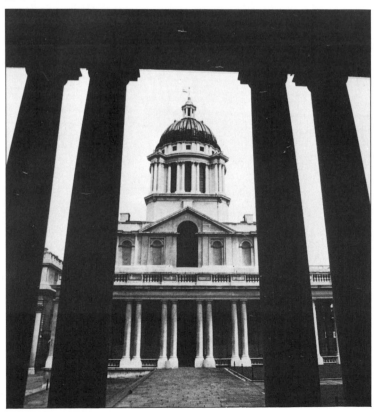

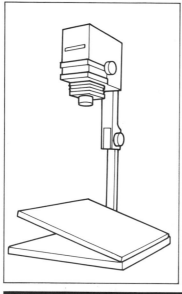

◀ The simplest way to correct converging verticals is to tilt the print paper by raising one side of the easel as shown. A similar effect can be achieved by tilting the enlarger head. Unfortunately, the scope for correction by this method is limited by depth of focus. On some enlargers you can increase depth of field when the easel is tilted by tilting the negative, lens and baseboard independently. By tilting the negative in the enlarger head one way, keeping the lens horizontal and tilting the easel the other, you can ensure all the image is in focus at quite steep angles.

▼ During printing I corrected the perspective to achieve this much more natural result by tilting the bottom of the picture up towards the enlarger lens to 'shrink' this end of the picture.

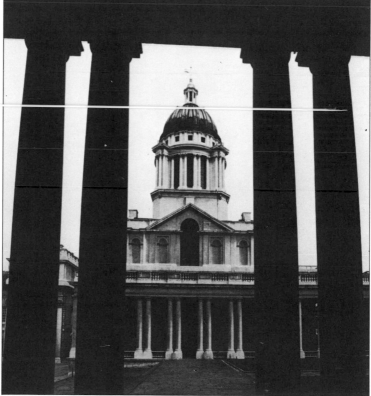

PREPARE FOR COLOR

Color processes have many similarities to black and white processes, and the equipment needed is substantially the same. However, all color processes need a far greater degree of precision in time and temperature control — essentially because there are three emulsions, not one, and inaccuracies in processing throw out the color balance. Precision is the key to success.

● **Use plastic tanks** for color processing if you can. Stainless steel tanks may be affected by certain color chemicals (notably bleach-fix solutions), and also take longer to empty, which can throw out timing of processes.

● **Measure temperature** with a mercury thermometer; spirit thermometers are just not accurate enough for color work. Alternatively, calibrate a spirit thermometer against a more accurate mercury thermometer (see below).

● **If you do much color work,** think about investing in a tempering unit to help ensure accurate temperature control.

● **Use different containers** for your color and b&w work if you can. Color chemicals are very strong and may contaminate the b&w solutions unless containers are cleaned with extreme care.

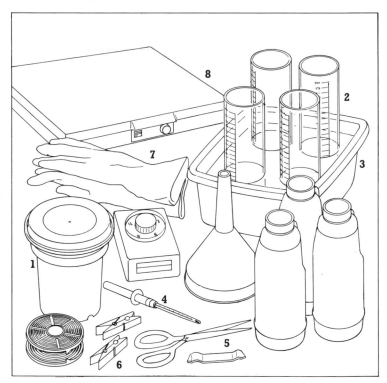

What you need:
1. Film processing tank
2. Graduates
3. Water bath for solutions
4. Precision thermometer
5. Scissors
6. Film clips
7. Rubber gloves
8. Tray warmer

Color negative process

Kodak C-41 process	Processing stages	Temperature	Time
	Color developer	37.8±0.15°C	3¼
	Bleach	24-40°C	6½
	Wash	24-40°C	3¼
	Fixer	24-40°C	6½
	Wash	24-40°C	3¼
	Stabilizer	24-40°C	1½
	Dry		10-20

Virtually all widely available color negative films can now be processed in Kodak's C41 chemicals, or in compatible chemistry from other manufacturers. Kodak, Fuji, Konica, and Agfa films are all processed C41, as are films from most of the 'own-label' manufacturers such as department stores. The processing sequence above is for Kodak's own Flexicolor process, but most makers of darkroom chemicals market a C-41 kit. Some of these independent kits are very cheap and easy to use, combining bleach and fix to cut down process times and stages. Remember to take care when handling color chemicals – some are very harmful. Wear rubber gloves, and ensure that all the bottles are properly labelled, and kept out of reach of children.

Color reversal (slide film) process

E-6 process	Processing stages	Temperature	Time
Kodak Ektachrome			
	First developer	38±0.3°C	6
	Wash	33-39°C	1½-3
	Reversal bath	33-39°C	1½-3
	Color developer	38±0.6°C	6-8
	Conditioner	30-40°C	2
	Bleach	33-39°C	6
	Fix	33-39°C	3-6
	Wash	33-39°C	1½-4
	Stabilizer	33-39°C	½-3
	Dry	below 60°C	

Most color slide films can be processed at home. The only major exception is Kodachrome, which requires a complex processing sequence generally available only at Kodak. Virtually all other films are processed in Kodak's E6 chemistry, or in comparable solutions from other manufacturers. The E6 process was originally conceived for laboratories with automated processing machines, so solution temperatures are high, and process times short. Though it isn't difficult to duplicate the process in the home darkroom, you need to take special care, and measure temperature and time with great accuracy. Additionally, the process itself is more complex, with two extra steps – first developer and reversal.

PROCESS COLOR NEGATIVES

The processing sequence for color negatives varies according to the kit you use, and it is important to follow the instructions to the letter. But with all processes, you need to pay meticulous attention to process times and temperatures and methodical agitation, especially during development. Unlike in b&w work, you cannot afford to ignore a ½° drop in temperature, or even the time it takes to fill and empty the tank. If you do not have a tempering bath to control temperature — and it is well worth getting one — make sure the average temperature is correct. In other words, if the developer cools down by 2° during processing, start with the temperature 1° (half of 2°) above the recommended temperature. Never stray more than ¼° with Flexicolor, though.

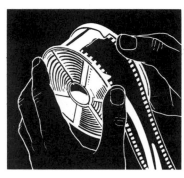

1 Load the film into the tank in total darkness in exactly the same way as for ordinary black and white film. Because color film is even more sensitive to fogging than black and white, check once again that your loading area is absolutely lightproof.

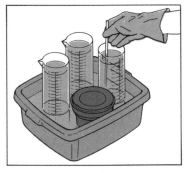

2 Mix the chemicals carefully according to the maker's instructions, taking care not to cross-contaminate the solutions. Number the containers in the order they are to be used and bring them and the developing tank to the right temperature in the water bath.

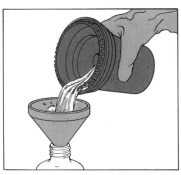

5 Drain the tank after the allotted time, pouring reusable developer back into the bottle. Then refill the developing tank with bleach at the correct temperature. Remember that development continues until the tank is full of bleach, so solution changes must be timed precisely.

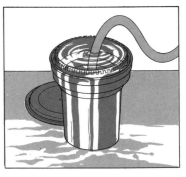

6 Bleach for the set time, then drain and wash in running water. You can take the lid off the tank to make washing easier if you wish. Remember to keep the water warm enough. After washing, check fixer temperature, pour the fixer into the tank and start timing.

● **Start draining** the developer a little before the time is up to allow for the time it takes to drain the tank.

● **Take care** not to splash chemicals. Rinse away splashes immediately to avoid damage and stains.

● **Adjust washing time** according to the water temperature, within the range 24°-40°C.

● **Use water from the water bath** for the first few rinses of each wash then gradually add cooler water. Be sure the water bath is not contaminated, though.

● **Never** let water drop below 20°C (68°F).

● **Don't worry** about the milky appearance of the emulsion when it is wet. This disappears as the film dries.

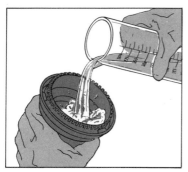

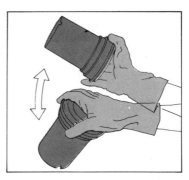

3 Check the temperature of the developer and adjust if necessary. Pour the developer into the tank quickly but smoothly and start timing immediately. Tap the tank sharply on the bench to dislodge air bubbles trapped on the film surface. Begin to agitate at once.

4 Agitate according to the maker's instructions, and then check the temperature of the developer in the tank. If this has dropped, work out how much you will need to extend development time to compensate. Stand the tank in the water bath between agitation.

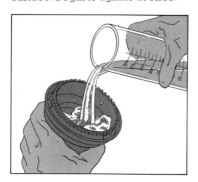

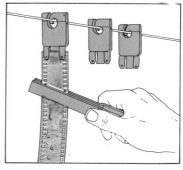

7 At the end of the allotted fixing period, drain the tank once more and wash in running water. Where specified, pour in the stabilizer and then dry without rinsing. Otherwise, give the film a final rinse in water treated with wetting agent.

8 Attach clips to the film and draw it from the spiral. Wipe dry very carefully and hang in a warm dust-free environment. Make sure that the temperature in the drying area does not climb above 45°C (115°F) or the emulsion may be damaged.

PROCESS COLOR SLIDES

Color slide film processing demands even greater precision perhaps than color negative processing. This is because the slide is the finished product and there is no opportunity to correct any minor faults during printing. Color slide film processing is also a little more complex, for it has two significant extra steps. Instead of going straight into the color developer which forms colored dyes in exposed parts of the image, color slide film is first developed to give a b&w negative image. This must then be 'reversed' to a positive before it can be color developed — hence the name 'reversal' film. In E-6 processing, this reversal is achieved chemically: earlier transparency processes reversed the image by exposure to white light.

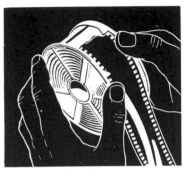

1 Load the film into the tank in total darkness in exactly the same way as color negative and black and white film. Once the film is safely in the tank, stand the tank in the water bath to warm it up to the correct processing temperature.

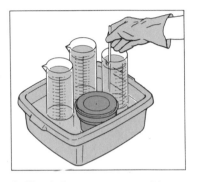

2 Check the temperature of the first developer solution and adjust if necessary. With the tank on the bench, pour in the developer and start timing. Tap the tank sharply on the bench to dislodge air bubbles and begin to agitate the tank.

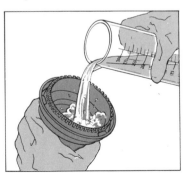

5 Check the reversal bath temperature — it should be within 2°C of the recommended temperature. Pour the reversal bath solution into the tank and agitate by inversion as recommended. This bath usually lasts about 2 minutes.

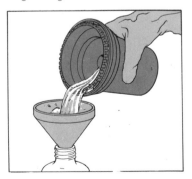

6 With P41 processes, place the spiral in a white bowl. Set a 150W bulb in a domestic lightfitting such as a desk lamp, a measured 1ft (30cm) from the spiral. Switch on the lamp for one minute. Switch off, turn the spiral over, and expose for a further minute.

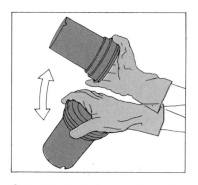

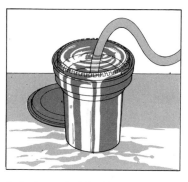

3 Agitate the tank according to the process instructions, replacing the tank in the water bath between agitation periods to stop the solutions from cooling. Monitor the temperature carefully during development, since errors will affect slide density.

4 At the end of the first development time, drain the tank swiftly, and fill with wash water. You can use running water, or water taken from the water bath. Temperature of wash water is less critical than that of solutions, but should still be within 3° of 36°C.

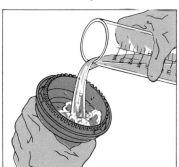

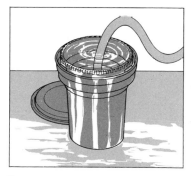

7 Check the temperature of the color developer and adjust if necessary. Pour in the developer and start timing. Tap the tank to dislodge air bubbles and agitate as indicated by the process manufacturers. Start draining the tank a little before time is up.

8 Pour in the stop, wash or conditioner as directed, drain and pour in the bleach bath. After bleaching, wash if necessary, then add the fixer. Wash in running water for the recommended time, rinse in stabilizer if directed, and dry normally.

71

PREPARE TO PRINT IN COLOR

Color printing is the most demanding of all the basic darkroom techniques, calling not only for very precise processing, but also fine control of the color of the enlarger light through the use of colored filters. Nevertheless, if you can handle black and white printing confidently, there is no reason why you should not try printing in color. Modern processes and paper have removed much of the scope for error in color printing, and you will soon find the extra control over color possible at home gives you prints much better than a commercial machine print can ever give.

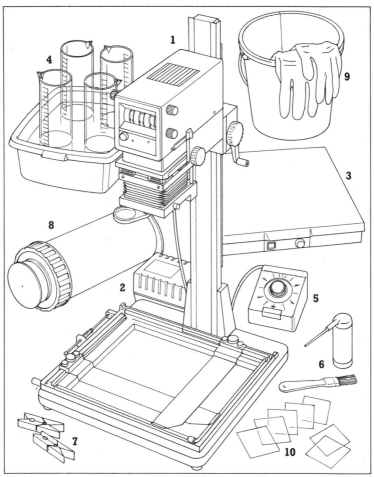

What you need

1. Enlarger with facilities for color filtration
2. Voltage regulator
3. Tray warmer
4. Bowl, graduates and precision thermometer (see page 66)
5. Timer
6. Brush and compressed air for cleaning negatives
7. Pegs
8. Print processing tube
9. Rubber gloves
10. Set of acetate filters if your enlarger has no color head

Prints from negatives

Kodak Ektaprint 2	Processing stages	Temperature	Time (mins)
	Presoak	30°C	½
	Developer	32.8±0.3°C	3½
	Stop bath	30-34°C	1
	Wash	30-34°C	1
	Bleach-fix	30-34°C	1½
	Wash	30-34°C	3½
	Dry	below 99°C	

Reversal prints from slides

Kodak Ektachrome R-3000	Processing stages	Temperature	Time (mins)
	Presoak	30°C	½
	First developer	30°C	2¾
	Wash	30°C	⅓
	Wash	30°C	⅓
	Wash	30°C	⅓
	Color developer	30°C	5¼
	Wash	30±2°C	⅓
	Wash	30±2°C	⅓
	Bleach-fix	30°C	4
	Wash (running water)	30±2°C	2¼
	Dry	below 99°C	

Cibachrome prints for slides

Processing stages	at 20°C (mins)	at 24°C (mins)	at 29°C (mins
Presoak	–	–	½
Developer	4	3	2
Rinse	½	½	½
Bleach	4	3	2
Fix	4	3	2
Wash	4	3	2

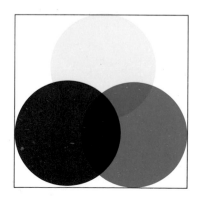

Color filters
Filters for color printing by the subtractive method come in yellow, magenta and cyan. A full strength filter in each color would subtract a third of the spectrum. The filters normally used, however, are much weaker than this. Their strengths are given in numbers up to 100 — a low number, eg 05, indicates a pale filter. The filters used for a particular negative are usually written in the order yellow, magenta, cyan, with the appropriate strengths.

TEST FOR EXPOSURE

In printing from color negatives, there are two variables to test for before you make each print: exposure and color balance. You should always test for exposure first because without correct exposure you cannot hope to achieve good color balance. In many ways, testing for exposure with color prints is similar to tests for black and white prints, and the simplest and most reliable method is to make a test strip covering a range of exposure times. However, before you make the test, you must make sure the enlarger light is roughly the right color by selecting the basic filter pack or dial-in filter setting given with the printing paper. This varies widely according to the film-paper combination from zero filtration to settings such as 50 magenta 90 yellow 0 cyan.

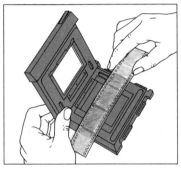

1 Dust your chosen negative and place it in the negative carrier with the emulsion (dull side) down. Switch on the enlarger and switch off the room lights. With the enlarger lens at full aperture, compose and focus the image on the easel in the normal way.

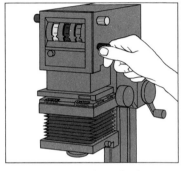

2 Consult the packet of print paper for the recommended starting filtration. If your enlarger has a dial-in color head, adjust the controls accordingly. If not, make up a filter pack, using as few filters as possible, and insert the pack in the filter drawer.

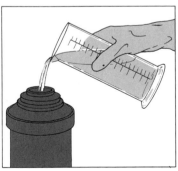

5 Prepare all the solutions and bring them to the correct temperature in a water bath. Fill the print tube with water at the presoak temperature. Leave for one minute, agitating occasionally to ensure all the print is warm, then drain the tube.

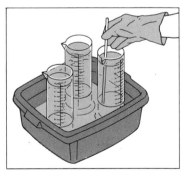

6 Check the temperature of the solutions and adjust if necessary. Pour the developer into the tube. Some tubes are filled upright for filling and processing begins when you lay them down. Other tubes are loaded lying down and processing starts when you roll them.

● **Use a UV filter** as well as the color balance filters.

● **Use a full sheet** of paper for the test unless your processing tube will take smaller sheets.

● **Identify the emulsion** side of the paper by its sticky feel.

● **Clean and dry the tube** thoroughly before loading the exposed print.

● **Process the same way** every time to ensure predictable results.

● **Keep the tube level** during processing or solutions may drain to one end.

● **Speed dry test prints** with a hair dryer, keeping the print cooler than 200°F (93°C).

● **With a rotary drum,** process under safelight until after fixing.

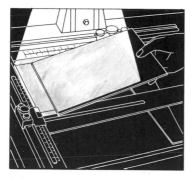

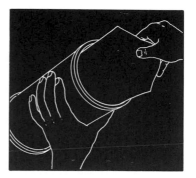

3 Stop down the lens to $f11$ and switch off the enlarger. In total darkness or under a Wratten 13 safelight, place a sheet of print paper on the easel. Make a test strip in the same way as for b&w prints, but move the card every five seconds up to a total of 25.

4 Gently curve the exposed paper and load it into the processing tube with the emulsion facing inwards. Seal the lid of the tube tightly and check that there is no unexposed paper lying uncovered. Switch on the room lights and prepare to process.

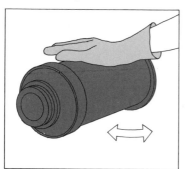

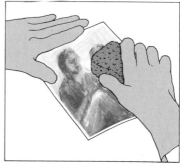

7 Lay down or roll the tube to start development. Start timing at once. Agitate by rolling the tube back and forth on the bench once every two seconds, or as instructed. Drain the tube, starting ten seconds before the end of the allotted time.

8 Repeat steps 6 and 7 for the stop and bleach-fix baths, then remove the print from the tube, handling it carefully by the edges. Wash in a tray under warm running water for the recommended time. Sponge water from the print to prevent drying marks. Hang to dry.

TEST FOR COLOR

When you are examining the test print to identify the right exposure time, you may notice that colors are not quite right. Only rarely does the starting filtration give perfect color balance. Usually, the first test print has a slight color cast, and the next step is to find what adjustments to filtration will neutralize this cast. This means making another test print, this time giving a range of filter combinations or settings rather than exposure times. To select the range of filtration, you must roughly identify the cast. If the colors in the first test print look warm, the cast is yellow, red or magenta. If they look cold, suspect a green, cyan or blue cast. For the color test, add a little filtration of the same color to the starting filtration, and try a range of close combinations.

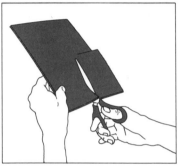

1 For the color test, divide the print into quadrants rather than narrow bands to ensure that each area is representative of the whole print. Start by cutting a quarter away from a piece of opaque card large enough to cover the entire print area.

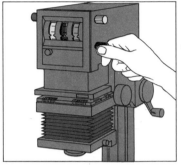

2 Write down the four different filter settings to be used in the test. Dial in the first new setting on the color head or make up a filter pack, using as few filters as possible — use one 20M filter rather than two 10Ms. Switch off the room lights.

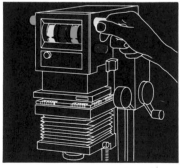

5 Take the print paper from the easel and store it somewhere lightproof. Switch on the room lights and dial in the filtration needed for the second part of the test or make up an appropriate filter pack. Work out the change in exposure needed.

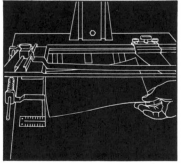

6 Switch off the room light and retrieve the partially exposed paper from its temporary storage. Replace the paper in the easel, using the snipped off corner to guide you. The paper must be in exactly the same position as it was for the first exposure.

● **Don't overdo filtration.** A ten unit change corrects most pale color casts.

● **To correct a warm cast,** try adding 10Y, 10Y + 10M, and 10M to the starting filtration. To correct a cold cast, try subtracting 10Y, 10Y + 10M and 10M.

● **Never combine** all three colors of filter. Instead, subtract the value of the weakest color from the values of the others.

● **Adjust the exposure** according to the recommended filter factors for each change in filtration.

● **Identify a cast** more precisely by looking at the first test print briefly through a range of filters. Once you find a filter combination that gives good color, note their values and then use half these values in the filter pack.

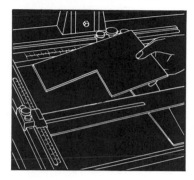

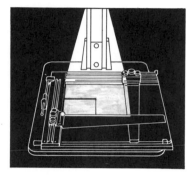

3 Take out a fresh sheet of paper and snip off one corner. This will help you to position the print the right way round for each part of the test. Place the paper in the easel and lay the opaque card in place so that all but one quadrant is masked.

4 Expose the first quadrant for the time determined by the exposure test, adjusted to take into account the new filtration. When the exposure is over, switch off the enlarger and lift the card. Lay it on the bench in exactly the same orientation.

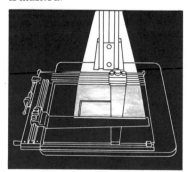

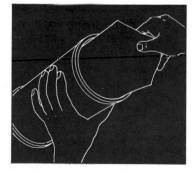

7 Flip the card mask over to uncover a new quadrant. Lay the card in position over the easel and make the second exposure. Repeat the procedure for the other two test quadrants, adjusting the filtration and exposure for each quadrant.

8 Process the color test print in the same way as the exposure test. When the print is dry, examine it in good, bright light. If no quadrant gives correct color, you must make a third test. Otherwise, you can make a full print, using the values, established by the tests.

BALANCE COLOR

Quadrant tests enable you to get fairly close to the filtration needed for correct color, but it can often be very difficult to make the next step and fine tune the color. The problem lies in identifying the color of the slight remaining cast. Cast identification becomes easier with experience, but for your early efforts at color printing, it is worth making a color 'ring-around' chart like the one below as a reference. The numbers below each print indicate the density of the filters needed to correct the cast.

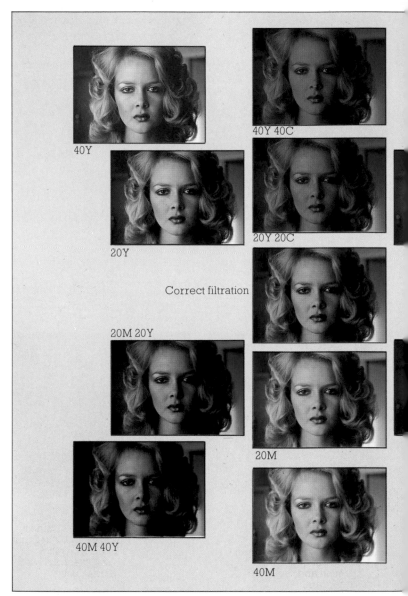

40Y

40Y 40C

20Y

20Y 20C

Correct filtration

20M 20Y

20M

40M 40Y

40M

● **Look for a second color.** Not all casts have a single color component. A print with a predominantly magenta cast may also have a slight red tinge as well, making the print orangey.

● **Find a secondary cast** by making a test print that corrects the predominant cast alone, then identifying the filtration needed to correct the remaining cast.

● **Remember** that to correct a red cast you need yellow and magenta filtration, for a blue cast magenta and cyan and for a green cast cyan and yellow.

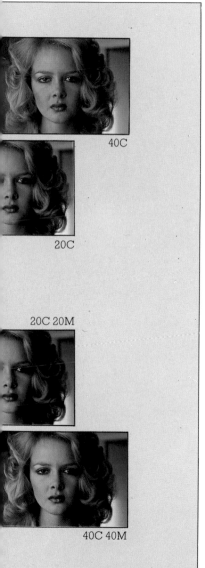

40C

20C

20C 20M

40C 40M

◄ A color ring-around provides an invaluable reference chart with which you can compare your test prints to help you identify a cast. The chart is essentially a series of prints made from a good, typical negative, each with a different but carefully controlled color cast. You can buy commercially-made ring-arounds, but making your own is one of the best ways of becoming familiar with color casts.

To make a ring-around, select a well-exposed negative with a good range of tones and colors, preferably including flesh tones, since these are particularly sensitive to color imbalances. From this negative, make a correctly-exposed, correctly color-balanced print and note down the filtration.

Starting with this filtration as a base, make a series of small prints, progressively changing the filter pack by 20 units for each of the six possible combinations of filters: yellow, yellow and magenta, magenta, magenta and cyan, cyan, cyan and yellow. Arrange these prints on white card in the manner shown and write down the filtration needed to correct the cast alongside. The filtration needed is simply the filtration you gave to create the cast removed. So where you gave 40Y 40M, for instance, the cast is corrected by subtracting 40Y 40M from the filter pack (or alternatively, adding 40C). The filters used here are Kodak.

To find the filtration needed to correct future prints, simply compare the test print with your ring-around chart. When you find an image in the ring-around that matches the test print in color, read off the filtration and adjust the filtration for the main print accordingly.

PRINT FROM SLIDES

To make prints from slides, photographers often used to copy the slide onto negative film to make an 'internegative'. This negative would then be printed in the normal way. Nowadays, however, it is just as easy to print the slide directly onto 'pos/pos' paper, so called because it gives a positive print from a positive original. Pos/pos paper is of two main types, reversal papers and Cibachrome. Reversal papers work in the same way as most other color processes, forming dyes during processing. Like color slides, the image is made positive by reversal processing. In contrast, in the Cibachrome process uniquely, dyes are present in the unexposed print and are destroyed selectively. The processing sequence below is for reversal papers.

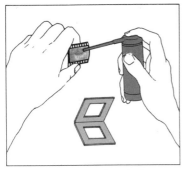

1 To make a print directly from a slide, remove the slide from its mount and clean it using a soft brush or a compressed air jet. Insert the slide into the negative carrier and place in the enlarger. Focus and compose the image in the usual way.

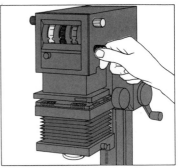

2 Set the starting filtration according to directions on the paper pack. Switch off the room lights and place a sheet of reversal paper on the easel in total darkness — there is no safelight for pos/pos papers. Place card ready for a test print.

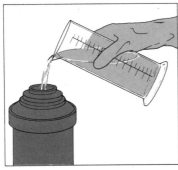

5 Pour in the first developer and start development. Agitate in the same way as for color negative printing. Begin to drain the tube 10 seconds before development is up. Give a stop bath if advised, then wash well in two minute-long baths of fresh warm water.

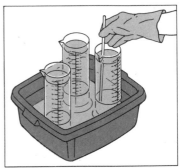

6 Check the temperature of the color developer and adjust if necessary. Pour the solution into the tube and start timing. Accuracy is vital, for it is in this stage that the silver negative image is reversed to a positive and the color dye image forms.

● **If the print is too dark,** increase exposure — opposite to prints from negatives.

● **Identify the cast** by comparing the test with the slide.

● **Correct color casts** when printing from slides by subtracting filters of the same color or adding filters of the other two colors. Change filtration in bigger units than with color negatives.

● **For Cibachrome prints,** the procedure is similar, though Ilford recommend a quadrant for all tests. But Cibachrome prints must be processed in their own chemicals in the following sequence: Developer (3 mins); rinse (30 secs); bleach (3 mins); fix (3 mins); wash (3 mins). Times are for processing at 75°F (24°C). Add or subtract half a minute from each stage for every 3°F above or below 75°F, up to 84°F (29°C).

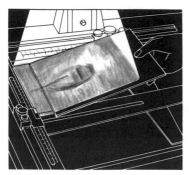

3 Make a series of test exposures in the same way as for color negative printing (see page 74-5). For an 8 × 10 print with a starting filtration of 45C 45M, make the test exposures at intervals of 2, 4, 8 and 16 seconds with the lens set at an aperture of $f8$.

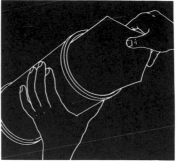

4 After exposing the test print, load it into the processing tube and turn on the lights. Fill the tank with warm water at the same temperature as the first developer. During the presoak, check the temperature of the first developer and adjust if necessary.

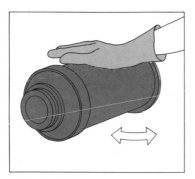

7 Agitate during color development by rolling the tank on the bench or, better still, using a motorized tube roller. After color development, wash briefly and pour in the bleach-fix. Then wash again, use a stabilizing bath if specified, then wash again.

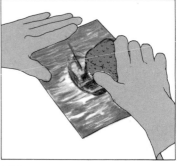

8 Wipe away excess water and dry as prints from negatives. When dry, select the exposure band and make a quadrant test (see page 76-7), adjusting filtration and exposure as above. Repeat until you have a perfect quadrant, then make the final print.

COMBINE SLIDE IMAGES

One great advantage of using color slide film is that the results are easy to manipulate. By sandwiching two slides together, you can see immediately what a combination image will look like. By comparison, combining images in the darkroom is more time consuming, and requires a greater degree of skill. Sandwiching isn't the only technique you can use: with a slide copier, such as the apparatus shown at the foot of the facing page, you can combine images additively – adding a setting sun, for example, to a lyrical landscape.

Sandwiching Slides
This is the easiest way to combine images on slide.

● **Pick thin images** – normal slides look too dark when sandwiched.

● **Choose just one main image** and use the other to add texture or color, or some other simple element. If both images are rich in detail, they'll compete.

● **Clean the slides** then fix them together as shown opposite.

▾ This image was created by sandwiching together two slides – the hang-glider was on one, and the sunset on the other.

Additive copying
With a slide copier, you can make two exposures, to record first one image, then a second, onto a single piece of film.

● **Pick one original** with a clear dark area – such as blue sky. Copy this in the normal way, then tension the camera's shutter without advancing the film.

● **The second slide** should have light detail only in the area that was dark on the first slide. By copying the second image, you'll drop the light detail from the second image into the dark area of the first slide.

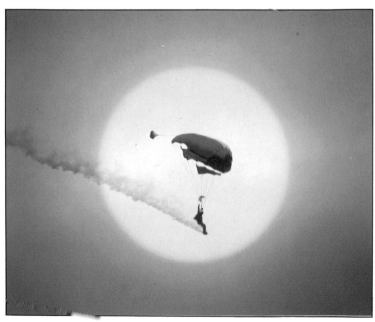

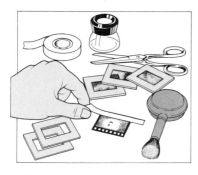

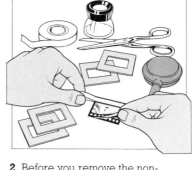

1 Start sandwiching by carefully cleaning both slides, and laying a strip of double-sided tape along the edge of the first image. Make sure that a sliver of tape does not intrude into the image area.

2 Before you remove the non-adherent backing from the tape carefully align the second image and check for positioning. Then peel off the backing, and press the two slides together.

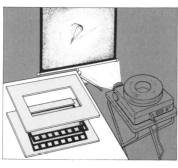

3 Finally, mount the slide in the normal way, ready for projection. Take care to secure the slide mount, because the two pieces of film may push apart the sides of a mount designed for just a single layer. The best mounts to use are those designed for audio-visual presentations. These slide mounts have glass cover plates that press the two images together, so that they both remain in focus when projected.

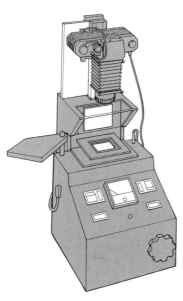

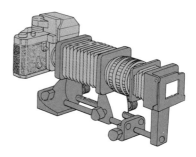

Slide Copiers
To combine images additively, you'll need a slide copier. The copier above fits onto the end of a bellows unit, and allows you to enlarge or reduce one or both elements of the combination. The sophisticated unit on the left has a number of additional features – you can control contrast of the combination, and exposure control is semi-automatic.

MAKE PHOTOGRAMS

You can make simple photographs called 'photograms' in the darkroom without even a camera. All you need is print paper, a light source — the enlarger is ideal — and a selection of objects to place in the light path. When the enlarger is switched on, the paper is exposed everywhere but in the shadow of the objects in the light path. So the paper records a negative image — a silhouette in reverse — of the object. Although the principle is simple, you can create some subtle and delicate effects by varying the position of the objects, the character of the light, and the paper.

● **Collect interesting shapes** for making photograms, or use everyday objects such as scissors, keys and coins. They should, ideally, be fairly flat.

● **Use black and white paper** for opaque objects, or else color the light source strongly.

● **Use any photographic material** you choose for translucent objects.

● **Plan your image in daylight.**

● **Set the aperture** at $f11$ and make a test strip, starting exposures at around ten seconds.

● **Process normally,** assess the test, and make a full photogram.

● **Try translucent objects** in the negative carrier.

● **Place small objects** in the negative carrier of your enlarger for the most exciting photograms.

● **For negative carrier photograms** place a glass plate or sheet of strong acetate in the carrier.

● **Focus the enlarger** with a small pin resting on the glass.

● **Suspend objects** that will not fit in the negative carrier in the lens housing, using cotton or clear tape.

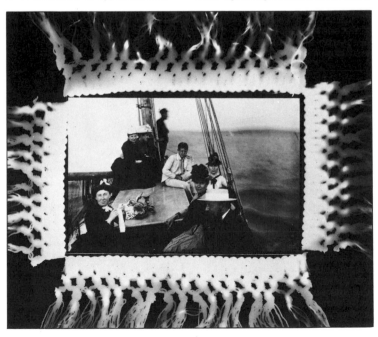

▼ This photogram was very easy to make and involved arranging cogs, punch tape, springs and various other objects on a piece of print paper under safelight, then exposing under the enlarger. However, to make a slightly more interesting photogram and give it a little depth, I printed on soft paper to retain mid-grey tones and shaded and dodged the photogram during exposure.

► Opposite, photogram techniques were used to create a border around a normal print.

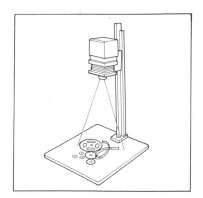

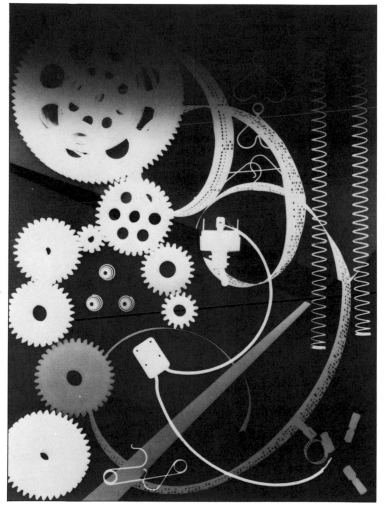

EXPOSE THROUGH GLASS

One of the easiest ways of adding interest to a black and white print is to retexture it during the printing process. Almost any material capable of passing light will lend a characteristic pattern to the image: you can print through tracing paper, a piece of stocking, or even lace curtains. The pictures on these pages were made by printing through various types of glass.

● **To soften an image,** place a sheet of diffusing glass just above or just below your enlarger lens. for part of the exposure.

● **To produce a pattern,** place a sheet of textured glass in contact with either the negative or the printing paper. Place the patterned side of the glass against the paper.

● **Experiment with color** printing paper and glass streaked with watercolor.

● **Smear petroleum jelly** on glass for a rippled effect.

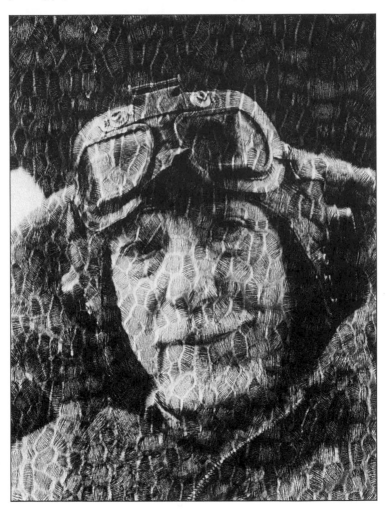

▶ The result of printing through the kind of rippled glass used to glaze bathroom windows was a pseudo-reticulation effect (opposite). A grained glass, similar to that used in diffusion screens, or as the focusing screens of view cameras, produced the image on the right; and a veined glass of the kind used to reduce strong directional light created the effect below. In each case, the sheet of glass was laid over the printing paper before the exposure was made. Although the overall impression was to be fairly soft, I decided to use a contrasty grade of paper, Grade 5. This helped to bring out the pattern of the glass very clearly and creates an effect reminiscent of a printer's half-tone screen.

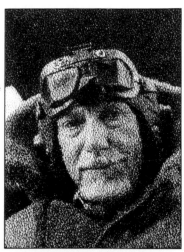

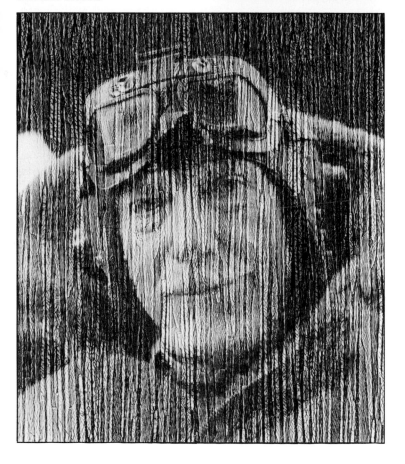

ELIMINATE TONES

By using lith film, you can eliminate shades of gray from a black and white print and create stark, graphic images from almost any negative. Lith film — a special material borrowed from the printing industry — is easy to use, and anyone who can make high quality black and white prints should have little trouble using this extremely high contrast material.

● **Use a red safelight** when working with lith film. Lith film may be fogged by the amber safelight usually recommended for ordinary printing paper.

● **Buy lith film in sheets,** or use it in 35mm rolls. 35mm film is noticeably cheaper but much less easy to use than 5 × 4 sheet film.

● **Use a special developer** such as Kodalith. This is packed in the form of dry crystals in two bags marked 'A' and 'B'. Make up two stock solutions by diluting each with water. Keep these separate until the moment you are

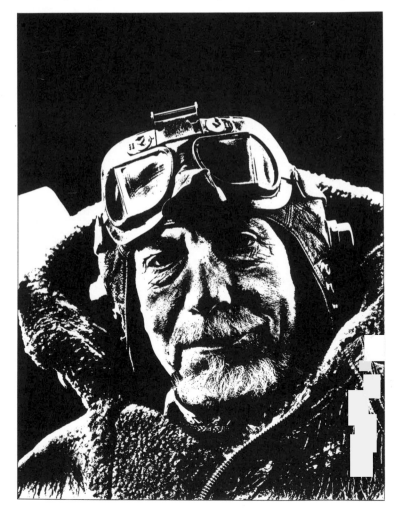

ready to develop the film.

● **Wear rubber gloves**
when handling lith chemicals.
They are very caustic and may
cause dermatitis.

● **Make up the developer** by
mixing stock solutions A and B in
equal parts.

● **Use the developer promptly** for
it deteriorates very rapidly. Once
it turns yellow, discard it.

● **Develop sheets of lith** film in
print processing trays for 2¾
minutes at 68°F (20°C). Handle the
film with rubber gloves rather than
tongs to avoid scratches.

◄ To eliminate the tones from the
original and create this rather
striking effect, I printed the
negative onto lith film under the
enlarger, retouching the image
with opaque dye where
necessary. I made a negative by
contact printing and then a
positive print from this.

● **Agitate continuously** for the
first two minutes, then leave still
through development.

● **Expose sheets of lith** under the
enlarger like ordinary prints.

● **Make a test strip** to find the
exposure, but use only small steps
(2, 4, 6, 8, 10, 12 seconds) for each
band because lith film has very
little exposure latitude.

● **To make a print,** expose the lith
positive in contact with another
sheet of lith to give a negative and
use this to print with, or . . .

● **. . . Print the positive** to give an
unusual negative image.

▼ I made this high contrast portrait
of the poet Robert Graves from a
black and white slide. To
eliminate the tones, I simply
exposed the slide in contact with a
short strip of 35mm lith film in a
contact proof printer. After
processing, I printed the resulting
lith negative in the normal way.

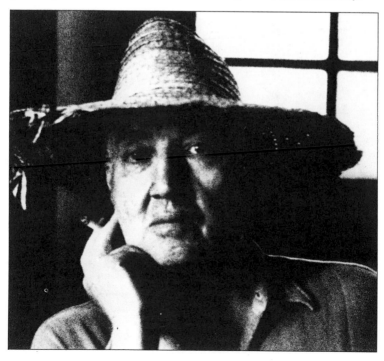

SOLARIZE IN B&W

One way of turning a fairly ordinary photograph into an attractive image is to solarize it. True solarization is difficult, but you can get much the same result using the Sabattier effect. The process, which involves exposing a print to light during development, is a little uncertain, so be prepared to experiment to get what you want and don't expect to be able to repeat it exactly.

● **Select a simple image** and make a normal print on Grade 5 paper for reference. Too complicated an image will yield a confusing print.

● **Make a second print,** but instead of developing it, put it away in a lightproof envelope or in a paper safe.

● **Remove the negative** from the enlarger. Using just white light from the enlarger, make a test strip (see page 54). Develop this for half the time that was needed to develop the reference print fully and completely.

● **Note the exposure** that gives a middle gray tone. This is the fogging exposure for the Sabattier effect.

● **Cover the enlarger** baseboard with a towel and place a dish of water on it.

● **Take the exposed sheet** of paper from its lightproof envelope and develop it for half the normal time. Then gently slide it into the dish of water, disturbing the surface as little as possible.

● **Let the ripples die away**

● **Fog the print** by switching on the enlarger for the time established by the test strip.

● **Complete development** by developing the print again for half the normal time.

● **Fix and wash** the print in the usual way.

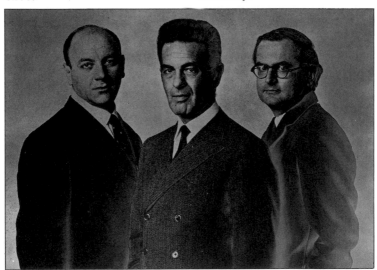

▲ Black and white film can be solarized in the same way as black and white prints, by contact printing onto lith film, developing for half the time, fogging with white light and completing development. A second way of solarizing a b&w print is to print onto high contrast paper and then re-expose to white light for a second or two halfway through development. Don't agitate.

▾ The solarized print of the model needed some supporting background. I chose the staircase first, then the image of the trees, overexposed about 100 times, was montaged onto the steps. Finally, I added the image of the duck so that there was an element in the foreground to lead the viewer's eye into the picture. Solarization of the entire image would have proved too confusing.

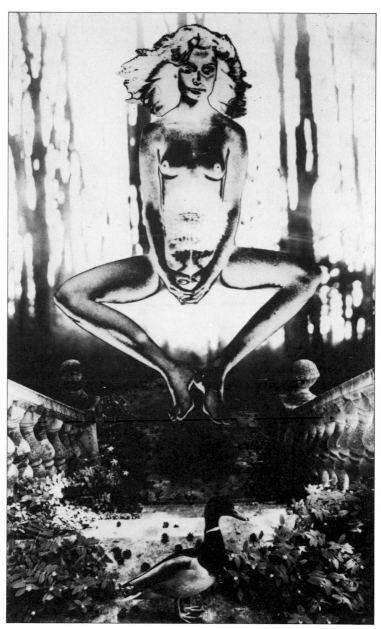

SOLARIZE IN COLOR

Sabattier effects can be even more startling in color than they are in black and white. Results are even less predictable than b&w solarizations — remember there are three emulsion layers not just one — but when they work, colors positively glow and pulsate. You can solarize color materials directly, but control is difficult and the failure rate high. For more controllable, and so cheaper, color solarizations, use solarized b&w transfer images.

● **Print the original** (color or b&w) onto lith film under the enlarger, making test strips.

● **Use panchromatic lith film** to record the reds in a color original, but work in total darkness.

● **Process the lith film** in lith developer but stop developing halfway through.

● **Fog the film** with a series of different exposures in a test strip running at 90° to the original strips.

● **Complete development** and look for best enlarger/fogging exposure combination. Use this to make a full lith film copy.

● **Contact the lith copy** onto continuous tone b&w darkroom film to make the transfer image.

● **Print the transfer image** either by itself or in a double-exposure print with the original onto color print paper. Color the exposing light by filtration.

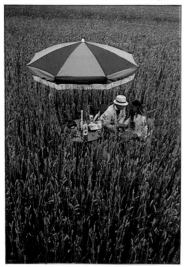

▲ To get the picture opposite, I printed the original slide (above) onto color negative paper, first straight for comparison (below) and then the final version which I fogged halfway through development with a bulb covered by a purple filter.

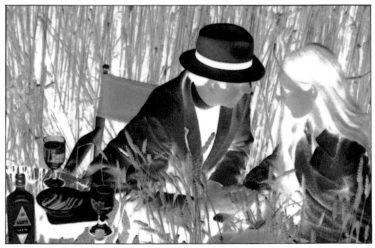

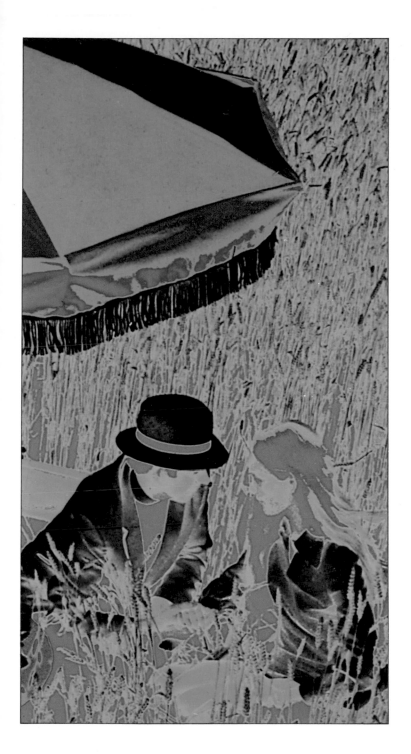

COMBINE PRINTS

Combining two or more pictures is a way of creating an entirely new image. The simplest method is to sandwich two negatives together in the enlarger, but multiple printing — exposing two or more negatives one after the other onto the same piece of paper — means you can print the second image at whatever size and in whatever position you want.

● **Plan the final image** on paper by projecting each negative in turn and tracing the outlines of the elements you want to use.

● **Use the tracing** as a hinged overlay so that you can size and focus each negative correctly.

● **Make a test print** for each negative.

● **Shade each image** during exposure with masks and dodgers cut to shapes that match the elements in the final print.

● **Add reflections** to a picture by printing the top half of the negative while masking off the bottom half of the print and then turning the negative through 180° and masking off the already exposed area of the print.

● **Use two enlargers** if you can, moving the masking frame from one to the other.

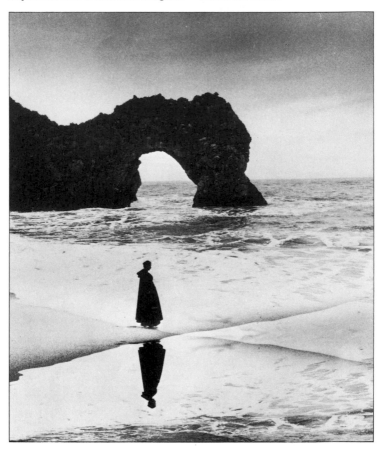

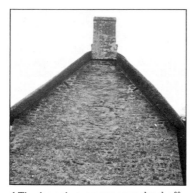

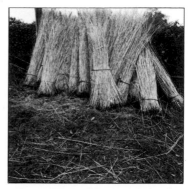

◄ The beach area was masked off and the image printed right way up. Then the negative was turned through 180° and the masking frame moved to print in the girl and the sea.

▲ The outlines of the cottage and the sheaves were traced on card. The cut card was used to mask, first, the area for the sheaves and then the area in which the cottage had been printed.

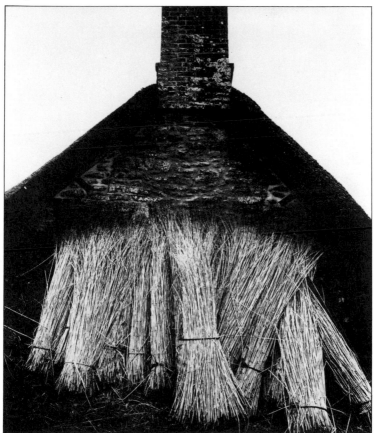

MONTAGE IN B&W

Few darkroom techniques provide more scope for creativity or just sheer fun than photomontage. By simply cutting out parts of some prints and sticking them down on another, you can create virtually any image you want. Bizarre, amusing, realistic, poignant — whatever you choose. Prints can be montaged in many ways, but there are two main approaches. Montages can either be 'rough cut' so that all the joins show up clearly, and there is no doubt that the picture is a montage. Or the joins can be hidden so that the picture seems to be just one photograph.

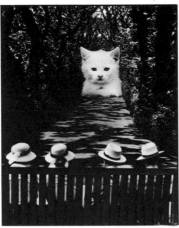

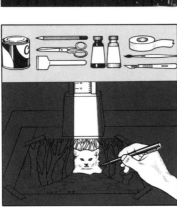

▲ This bizarre image was created by montaging two prints with invisible join techniques. After making a print of the park background, I traced in the cat's head and made a print on single weight matt paper to the right size. I then cut a rough outline, scored accurately around the cat's head, and carefully tore away the excess before pasting in place.

▼ I photographed this sequence with a montage in mind. All kinds of motordrive shots can work well when montaged together.

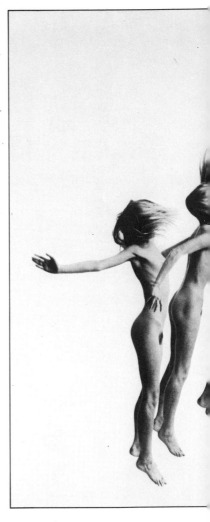

● **Lay tracing paper** over a large print of your background and draw in the outlines of the new elements.

● **Transfer the tracing** to the enlarger baseboard to make prints to the right size.

● **Match print characteristics** — paper grade, exposure and elements such as perspective — if you want invisible joins.

● **Cut a rough outline** leaving an inch to spare around the subject.

● **Scalpel along** the outline. Make a series of right-angle cuts from the outline to the score mark.

● **Gently tear away** the rough outline. Then sandpaper away unwanted fibers. Darken the edges with a soft pencil.

● **Stick the cut-out** down in place on the background print, pressing from the center out.

● **Retouch any weak areas** then photograph and reprint the finished montage.

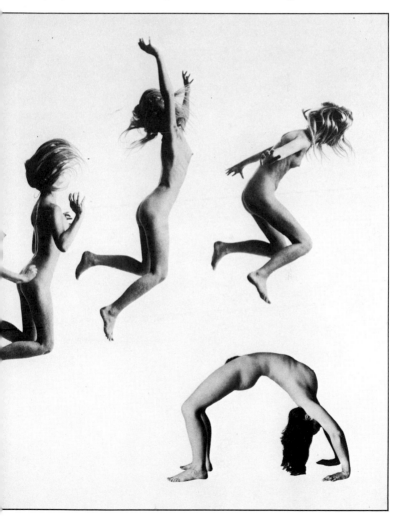

MONTAGE IN COLOR

Montage in black and white can produce fascinating results, but the additional dimension of color gives you even more scope to create strange and intriguing images. Color prints are far more expensive than black and white, though, and it is important to cut waste to a minimum by carefully planning each image in advance.

● **Color print papers** are now all of the RC type, so extra care is needed when montaging and it is important to use water-based dyes rather than oils when retouching to disguise joins.

● **Match color carefully** even if you are trying to create a bizarre effect. Any slight differences in color bias will show up badly. Use the same batch of paper for each print if you can.

● **Mix color and b&w** to draw attention to selected areas.

● **Use color negative film** as a starting point, rather than color transparencies. Negatives allow you much more control over the color and density of the finished print, so it's easier to match up each of the elements in the montage.

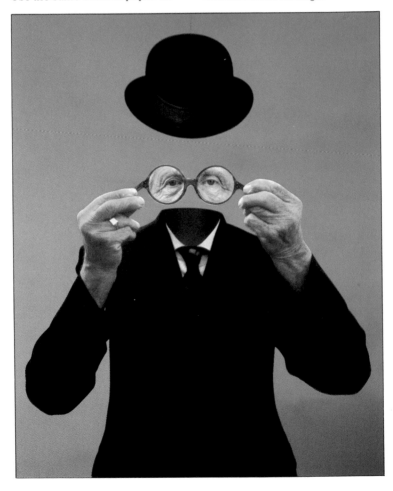

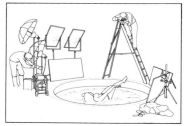

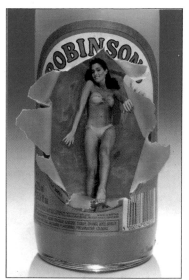

▲ Two separate pictures — a girl in a pool of orange-colored water and a bottle with a torn label — were taken specifically for this montage suggesting healthy living.

◄ Just two ideas for surreal montages in color. There are three elements in the headless man — a hat suspended on a cord, the man's face behind glasses, and his body. The car includes a pale upside down print.

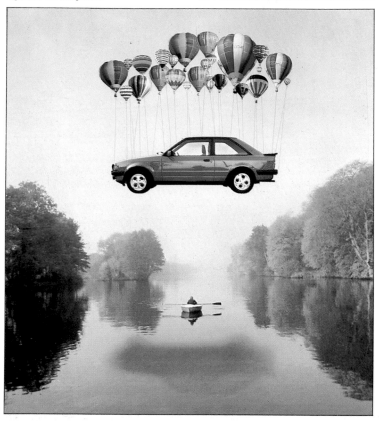

MONTAGE PATTERNS

Montage normally involves creating a picture by sticking to-gether different images. Yet one of the attractions of photography is the way you can reproduce the same image again and again. You can exploit this unique ability to create arresting patterns by montaging repeated images. The individual images are best printed separately since this gives the most scope for variation within the pattern. But if your pattern is to be symmetrical, and the idea of making 150 prints is daunting, try the shortcut suggested.

● **Plan the pattern** carefully in advance, using graph paper.

● **Print on Grade 5 paper** and maximize contrast — the pattern may not stand out with soft prints.

● **Create a sense of perspective** by 'overlapping' the images — that is, cropping more and more from each successive print.

● **Print 'distant' images lighter** and less contrasty in perspective images like that below to enhance the sense of depth.

● **A shortcut** in printing the images for symmetrical patterns is to print a few small images, montage them, copy the montage and make as many prints as you need from the copy.

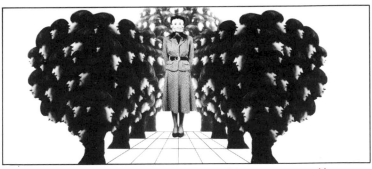

▲ I made this bizarre avenue by making a series of prints of the girl's head, some reversed, some not, and montaging them on artboard. Lines were ruled in ink.

▼ This frieze was created by printing the same shot four times and montaging the prints. By cropping a little more from each print, I created an overlap.

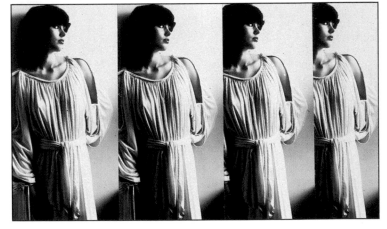

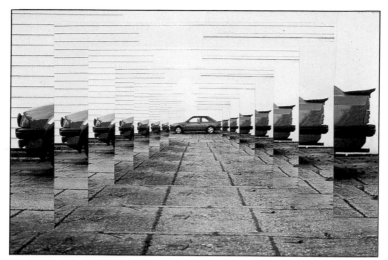

▲ I made this hall of mirrors by making eight prints of the car, of decreasing size, (the smallest slightly paler). The image was carefully planned to ensure straight perspective lines.

▼ This multiple portrait involved making 121 individual prints of the original image on Grade 5 paper and sticking them all painstakingly on art board and then photographing the result.

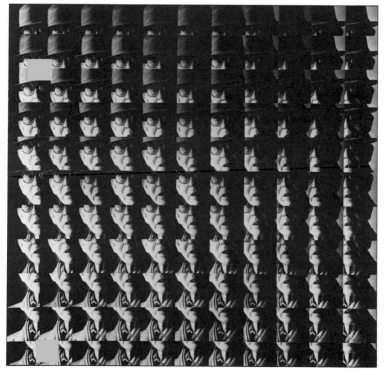

COMBINE TECHNIQUES

By combining some or all of the techniques outlined in the previous pages, you can create highly original images or pictures that match the slick fantasy images of the advertising world. Montage and airbrush techniques complement one another especially well, for the soft spray of the airbrush helps to blend the most unlikely elements into a colorful and coherent picture.

● **Plan your images** carefully. Materials are expensive, and any waste is costly.

● **Work as large as you can** afford. Large prints and boards are easier to work on, especially for fine detail. And blemishes and mistakes will be disguised when the finished piece is copied and reproduced at a smaller size.

● **Keep the lighting 'realistic',** however dramatic the effect you want. If the lighting looks impossible, the effect will be ruined.

● **Take stock shots** of attractive sunsets, dramatic skies, rising moons and other subjects that may be useful for montages. Remember to keep shots plain and uncluttered by irrelevant detail.

● **Build up the picture** in stages. Start by printing the background to the right size. Montage the different elements in place. Then, with the aid of masks, create the right finish with an airbrush.

● **Skies darken higher up.** Remember this when airbrushing.

● **Keep the airbrushing subtle.**

● **Photograph** the finished artwork and use the photograph to make a straight print. Put the original safely away. Making a copy print protects the delicate original and helps to disguise traces of your handiwork.

▶ I built up the flying car from three picture elements: a straight shot of a car in soft studio lighting; a landscape including half a rainbow, printed right and wrong way round to make a complete rainbow; and a 'vapour trail' added with an airbrush.

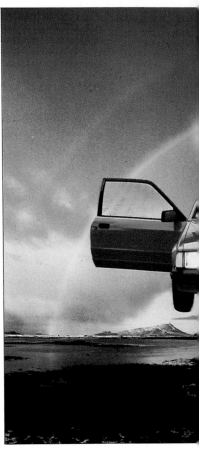

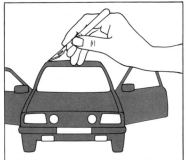

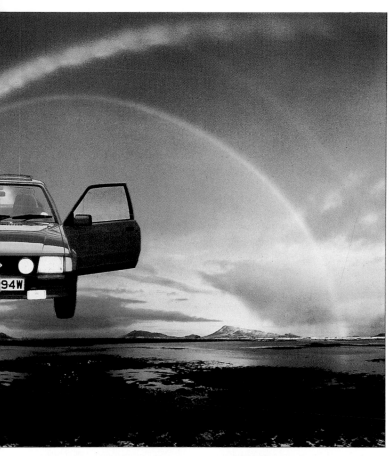

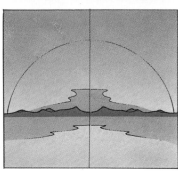
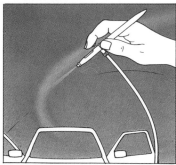

RETOUCH PRINTS

Retouching is one of the most valuable of all darkroom skills. By careful retouching, you can rescue prints blemished by dust spots and scratches, blotchy tones and even unwanted detail. You can also positively improve the image by bringing up some tones and playing down others. Retouching can never be a substitute for proper care in printing and your first task is always to get the best possible print. But, with practice, you can darken or lighten any part of the image you wish to make a print fit for mounting and presentation.

● **Retouch on fiber-based papers** rather than rc papers.

● **Don't handle the print.** As you work, protect it with a sheet of tracing paper.

● **Soak the print** in water to which wetting solution has been added before bleaching.

● **Lay the print down** onto a firm, waterproof surface.

● **Lighten large dark areas** by swabbing them with cotton wool soaked in Farmer's reducer. Then wash the print thoroughly.

● **Deal with mistakes** by mopping up with a wet sponge or by washing the whole print.

● **Lighten small areas** with a fiberglass pencil or a small paintbrush filled with reducer.

● **Remove tiny dark spots** by scraping them away with a scalpel blade (see below left).

● **Fill in white spots** on a dry print with a lead pencil or with a fine paintbrush filled with photo-dye or watercolor. Build the color up in stages until its density is correct (see below right).

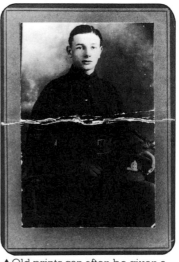

▲ Old prints can often be given a new lease of life with retouching skills. but don't retouch on the original; make a copy first. Not only does this allow for mistakes, it has the advantage that as you make the copy, you may be able to eliminate yellow stains by photographing through a blue filter. The picture above was torn in two when found, so I mounted the two halves on card and photographed it in the enlarger (see page 114).

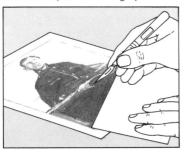

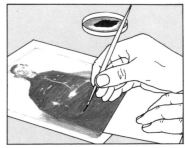

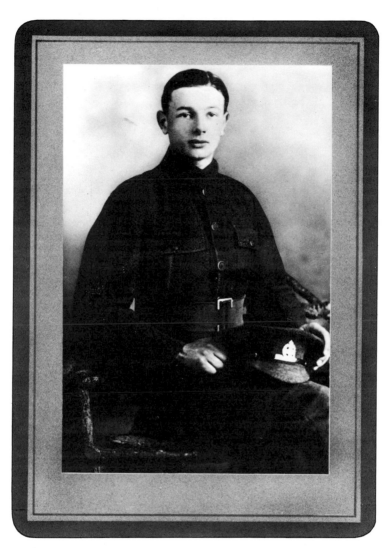

▲ From the copy negative of the torn original I made a print on unglazed fiber paper and worked on this. Although the final print was to be fairly small, I made this work print on 10 × 8in paper so that any errors would be reduced in size in the final print. All the tiny scratches were disguised by spotting with a fine-brush and water-color paints. The crack across the original was sprayed with an airbrush (see page 108-9). The background was still blotchy, so I carefully wet the area and swabbed with Farmer's Reducer on cotton wool to clean it up. I then rephotographed the retouched print and made the final print. This kind of restoration work is well worth doing if you are intent on building up an historical album. The negatives of many early photographs have been lost and they exist now only as damaged or dog-eared prints. Retouching helps to preserve bygone days for those to come.

COLOR BY HAND

Coloring black and white prints by hand is one of the simplest and cheapest of all darkroom techniques. Yet the subtle, pastel hues that can be achieved and the fine control over color is unmatched. By skilful hand-coloring, you can breathe delicate life into a gray print; highlight different parts of the picture; or create an entirely new image.

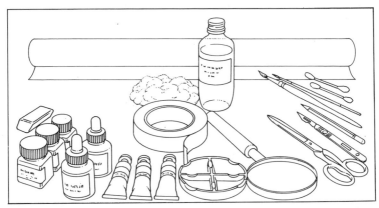

▲ For successful hand-coloring you will need some of these items: rubber masking lacquer; dyes; inks and tubes of color; a small sponge; a mixing palette; spirit for oils; a magnifier; scissors; scalpel; a range of brushes; cotton wool; pieces of blotting paper.

● **Make the print** on fiber-based paper, rather than RC. RC prints absorb even water colors poorly. Use matt paper rather than glossy. Large areas of color may be blotchy on gloss paper.

● **Underexpose** and underdevelop the print slightly, and print on fairly soft paper — the best prints for hand-coloring are usually rather flat and light since dark tones tend to overwhelm the color.

● **Sepia-tone prints** for a slightly more natural, warmer look to hand-colored prints. Or make the print on warmer-toned chlorobromide paper.

● **Use any coloring material** you choose — water colors, dyes, oil colors, felt tip pens, colored pencils or even food dyes. Oils give a more professional look.

● **Use proper photographic dyes** for your first experiments. They will reproduce on film just as they are seen by the eye.

● **For bright, vivid colors,** use water-based retouching dyes.

● **Soak the print well** in water before you apply water-based retouching dyes. Wipe away excess water with a squeegee. Tape down the wet print to prevent it curling as it dries.

● **Dilute the dyes** with plenty of water to give a very weak tint.

● **Color large areas** with a wide brush or a cotton wool swab, building up the color gradually layer by layer.

● **Work quickly** so that large areas are not left half-colored as the print dries.

● **Keep blotting paper to hand** to absorb running colors.

● **Mask adjacent colored areas** with rubber masking solution.

● **Use finer brushes** and less dilute colors on a dry print for details.

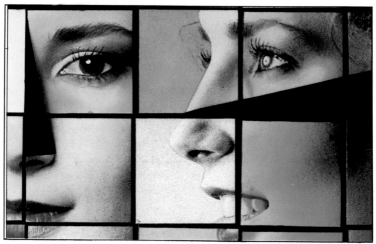

▲ Water-based dyes were used to color this composite print. Once each area was colored, it was masked with rubber solution while color was applied to new areas.

▼ Hand-coloring is particularly effective at giving a period look to a print — provided the subject is right. Here, water-colors highlight the old-fashioned handcart and milkman.

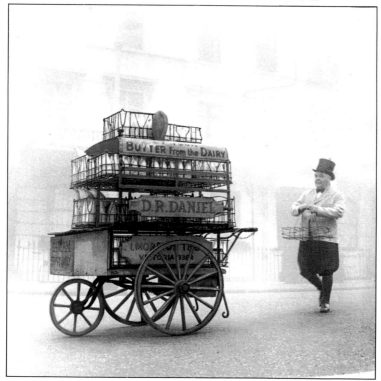

USE AN AIRBRUSH

Airbrushing is a difficult technique, but once mastered it allows you to make dramatic changes to prints and give your montages a slick, professional look. With an airbrush, you can eliminate unwanted backgrounds, add color where you want, retouch to hide cracks or joins in montages or even create an entirely new picture. An airbrush is basically a spray gun that delivers paint in a fine controllable spray. Some are powered by a compressor; some use just an aerosol can. But they are both used in much the same way.

● **Load the color** reservoir of the airbrush with a hoghair brush. Use grit-free paint: eg, gouache.

● **Adjust the air pressure** to suit the paint (follow the makers' instructions).

● **Hold the brush** like a pencil at an angle of 45°. Keep your index finger on the control button.

● **Start to spray** by first pressing the control to start the air flow and then pulling it back to release the color.

● **Control the spray** by balancing the air and color flow

● **Practise on paper** and then an old print.

● **Spray in parallel strokes** in one direction only, stopping the color at the end of each stroke.

● **Always use masks** when airbrushing, there is no other way of controlling where color goes.

● **Remove unwanted color** in a color print by airbrushing with white paint and then building up the desired color on top.

● **Protect** delicate airbrushed prints by rephotographing them (see page 114).

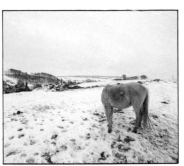

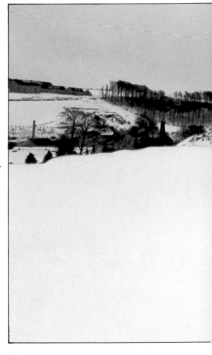

▲ In the original 35mm transparency of the hose, the snow around was well-trampled and unattractive. I made a 8 × 10in (20.3 × 25.4cm) color negative and then deleted the entire snow area with black dye. On a positive of the same size I then airbrushed in the unblemished snow.

▶ The final print both emphasize the horse's shape and creates a minor mystery — how did the horse get there in the first place when there are no hoofprints in the surrounding snow?

▶ To remove detail from a large and complex area of a print, you must use an adhesive mask. Lay the film for the mask over the entire print and its mount. With a sharp, new scalpel blade, carefully cut through the film around the area you want to spray. Be very careful to avoid cutting the print as well. When cutting round dark areas, err a little on the dark side of the tone boundary or you will get a 'halo' effect. Once you have cut out the area to be sprayed, peel the film away carefully. You are now ready to start airbrushing. Start by spraying the area evenly in a color that matches the surrounding area. Build up the color in smooth strokes, overlapping half the stroke each time. Be very sparing in your use of color. If in doubt, spray thin, wait until it dries, and go over the area again. When you have an even tone, you can begin to add detail if you wish. In skies, for instance, you could add white, fluffy clouds. Practice the effect on waste paper first, though.

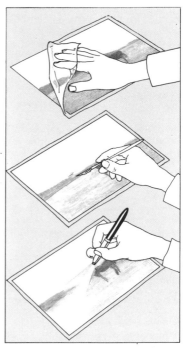

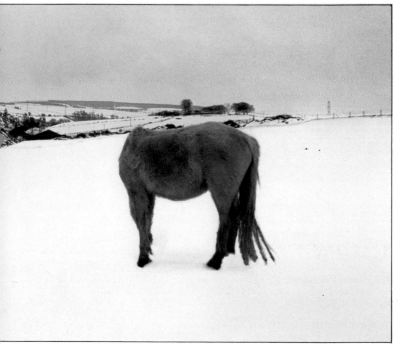

TONE B&W PRINTS

Toners enable you to add color or mood to a black and white print. The best known is sepia, which lends prints an air of antiquity; blue toner gives them the chill of winter; and you can extend the technique to produce multi-colored prints in which the colors can be as true or as creatively unnatural as you care to make them. Most toners are available in ready-to-use packs.

Sepia toning

Sepia toning gives prints a rich brown color and entails converting the metallic silver image to silver sulphide, which is more stable and permanent.

● **Ensure** that the room is adequately ventilated: the toning solution smells like rotten eggs and is highly toxic.

● **Use fiber-based papers** for prints you intend to sepia tone. The process softens contrast and brings out shadow detail, so you must adjust printing to suit it.

● **Soak dry prints** in water for half an hour before toning.

● **Immerse the print** in a bleaching solution of potassium ferricyanide and potassium bromide until the black metallic silver of the image has completely changed to pale yellow silver bromide.

● **Wash the print** for about five minutes until all traces of yellow have disappeared.

● **Filter the water** for the toner if it contains impurities.

● **Immerse the print** in the sodium sulphide toning solution, rocking the dish continuously until no further change in color can be seen.

● **Wash the print** for 10 minutes in running water.

● **Dispose** of the toning solution, which is dangerous, down an outside drain.

Blue toning

Iron toning, which consists of converting the mtallic silver to a ferrocyanide salt, gives a dark blue-toned print.

● **Use resin-coated paper.**

● **Underexpose the print** a stop so that the toner brings it up to normal intensity.

● **Make the toning bath** from two stock solutions. Mix them without dilution before use.

● **Prewash the print** for about an hour.

● **Use a hypo clearer** to ensure the print is clean.

● **Immerse the print** in the toning solution and rock the dish until the desired depth of tone is achieved.

● **Wash the print** for three to four minutes.

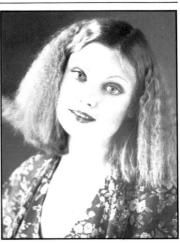

▲ This print was made by bleaching a black and white print and then redarkening it in a blue toner. Blue toners generally darken and intensify the print, so the original print was deliberately under-exposed and underdeveloped.

Dye coupler toning

Dye coupler toning exploits color chemistry to color b&w prints in a range of striking colors. It involves bleaching the silver print image back to the original silver halides and then redeveloping it in color developer. To the developer, special color couplers are added that 'couple' colored dyes to the silver so that it is combined with a colored dye image.

● **Soak the print well.**

● **Bleach** in standard bleach, then wash for 10 minutes.

● **Mix the color developer** and add the chosen coupler.

● **Immediately develop** the print until the color is right.

● **Rinse thoroughly.**

● **Briefly stabilize** the print.

▼ A mixture of yellow and cyan color couplers was used to produce this dye-coupled print. The second bleach-fix bath, which removes the silver, leaving only the dye, was omitted in order to give the picture a fuller image.

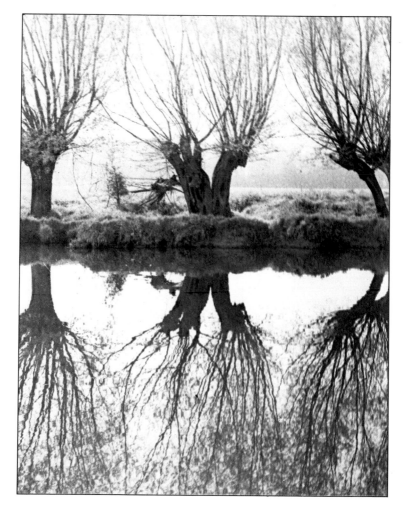

PRINT ON ANY SURFACE

With the aid of liquid emulsion, you can print photographs onto virtually any surface you choose. You can print pictures on plates, blocks of wood, stones, eggs — almost anything small enough to fit in your darkroom. Liquid emulsion, available in kit form and as the commercial product Liquid Light, is simply painted onto the surface under safelight, exposed and processed normally.

● **Choose your image** to match the surface you wish to print on. A picture of a chicken might go well on an egg, and so on.

● **Analyze the surface** of the object you wish to print on. Some surfaces need careful preparation or 'subbing' before they can be coated with emulsion.

● **Prepare non-porous surfaces,** such as glass and glazed ceramics by first cleaning very thoroughly with hot washing soda.

● **Sub glass and glazed ceramics** by coating them with a five per cent solution of gelatin, warmed in a bowl of water until it goes on easily.

● **Prepare cloth and paper** by cleaning thoroughly to remove any traces of chemicals.

● **Coat the back of paper** with five per cent gelatin solution to prevent it curling.

● **Seal wood and clay** and other porous surfaces with a polyurethane varnish to prevent the emulsion soaking in unevenly.

● **Seal surfaces** that might react the emulsion by coating with polyurethane varnish. This includes metal surfaces containing brass and iron.

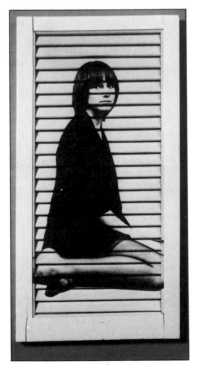

◀ At first sight, printing directly onto such a large surface as this louvred door seemed to be a daunting task. But in the event it proved to be quite straightforward, since I was able to take the door off its hinges and carry it to the darkroom, to work on. The surface needed no preparation apart from thorough cleaning, for the paintwork provided a perfect subbing layer. I tilted the enlarger head to give a large enough image and focused on a piece of old print paper taped to the door. I then coated a few small strips of similarly painted wood with liquid emulsion under safelight and made a few test exposures. With the exposure time established, I sensitized the door by filling a household plant spray with liquid emulsion and sprayed it over the surface. I then made the exposure and processed the image by swabbing down with a sponge soaked with all the chemicals in turn. An old plastic washing-up bowl made an ideal 'developing tray' and neatly caught all the drips.

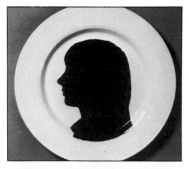

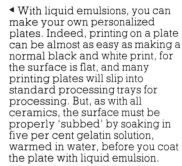

◄ With liquid emulsions, you can make your own personalized plates. Indeed, printing on a plate can be almost as easy as making a normal black and white print, for the surface is flat, and many printing plates will slip into standard processing trays for processing. But, as with all ceramics, the surface must be properly 'subbed' by soaking in five per cent gelatin solution, warmed in water, before you coat the plate with liquid emulsion.

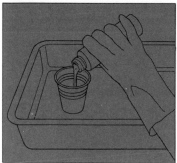

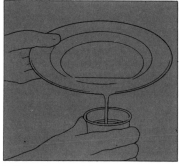

1 Melt the emulsion by placing your storage bottle in a hot water bath — not over direct heat. You will have to judge the quantity you need to cover the plate. Try to avoid pouring too much — it is expensive, and you may fog any emulsion returned to the bottle.

2 Pour the emulsion on to the warmed plate. Use rubber gloves to hold the plate. Spread your hand over the underside to avoid thumb marks, and roll the emulsion around to get an even coating. Work quickly in case the emulsion coagulates.

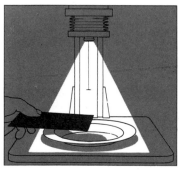

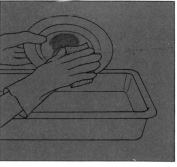

3 Liquid emulsion is easy to remove by washing in hot water and scrubbing gently, so you can make a series of test exposures on the plate in the same way as prints on paper. Once you know the correct exposure, wash off, recoat the plate and make the full print.

4 Process the plate as you would a print. You will need to extend the fixing time, using an acid hardener fixer. Handle the plate carefully as the emulsion will remain soft until thoroughly dry. Wash gently in tepid water. Finally, dry off and varnish with polyurethane.

COPY PICTURES

An enlarger makes a wonderfully versatile and high quality copying machine, and it is well worth learning how to exploit it as a copier, for copying is an integral part of many advanced dark-room techniques. Enlargers can be used for three main copying procedures, though not all enlargers are equally suitable for each. First, and most significantly, the enlarger can be used to copy negatives and slides onto sheet films in much the same way as for printing onto paper. Second, it can be used as a copy camera to photograph flat artwork, such as completed montages. Finally, it can be used, in conjunction with a camera, to make high quality duplicates of slides.

Copying onto sheet film

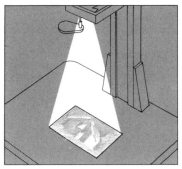

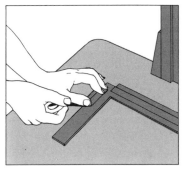

1 Place the slide or negative to be copied in the enlarger negative carrier and compose and focus the image as for normal printing (page 52). The size depends on the size of the sheet film — typically 5 × 4in.

2 Mark the edge of the image on the enlarger baseboard — the easel may be awkward to use — and then tape strips of black card down to make stops against which you can register the film in complete darkness.

Flat copying

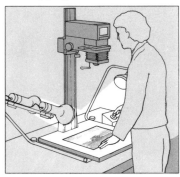

▲ Some enlargers are especially designed for easy transformation into copy cameras. This one has a reflex focusing screen, a film carrier that takes 35mm film in a light-tight package, and a copy stand equipped with lights.

● **Use the focusing screen** if your enlarger has one. Otherwise . . .

● **Focus** by projecting a negative onto the baseboard the same size as the image you wish to copy.

● **Use the film carrier** if your enlarger has one. Otherwise . . .

● **Place a sheet of film,** bigger than the negative masks, in the negative carrier in darkness. Seal the carrier with opaque tape.

● **Light the image** with proper copying lights. Otherwise . . .

● **Light the image** by moving a lamp held at 45° across the surface during exposure.

Calculate exposure from tests.

● **Use the masks** in the negative carrier to cut down flare. This is more important with copying work than it is with straight printing.

● **Use black paper** under the film during exposure if the baseboard of your enlarger is white. Reflection from the baseboard can cause halation.

● **Don't handle the film** any more than absolutely necessary.

● **Make sure** the emulsion is at the top when you place the sheet of film under the enlarger.

● **Tape the register stops well** to ensure the film cannot slip underneath.

● **Copies on color sheet film** can be made in exactly the same way, but you must work in total darkness and take much greater care.

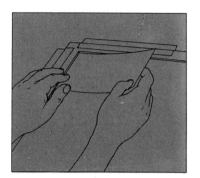

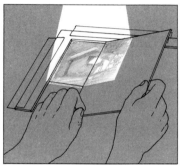

3 Under safelight, if you are using orthochromatic film, or in total darkness if you are using panchromatic film to make copies from color originals, slide the sheet film against the card, with the notch bottom left.

4 Make a series of test exposures in exactly the same way as for ordinary black and white prints. Process in a color print tube. Find the correct exposure and repeat the procedure to make the full copy.

Duplicating slides

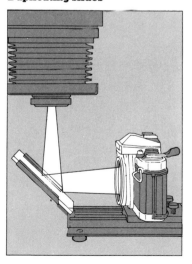

● **The simplest way** to duplicate slides using an enlarger is to remove the lens from a 35mm SLR and place it under the enlarger. The slide is then projected in the enlarger directly into the aperture of the SLR. Unfortunately, since you cannot use the camera viewfinder, it is difficult to compose the image.

● **The best arrangement** is with a front-silvered mirror held at an angle of 45° beneath the lens to reflect the image into the camera. Purpose-built stands with a rigid bracket for the camera are available.

● **Use filters** or the dial-in color head of the enlarger to control the color of the light.

WORK IN REGISTER

Many darkroom techniques involve separating an image into various elements — tone separations, color separations, contrast masks and many others. These elements are then re-united for the final print. If the image is to look sharp, the elements must be perfectly aligned. It is possible to 'register' the images visually in good light, but in dim light or total darkness it is impossible.

● **The best method** of registration is a punch system. This involves making two or more holes near the edge of each sheet of film or paper, in exactly the same place. The images are registered by slotting the holes over corresponding pins.

● **Register separations** made from a single negative onto sheet film under the enlarger by punching holes in each sheet before exposure. Tape a set of register pins to the enlarger baseboard and locate the film on the pins for each exposure.

● **Keep contact copies registered** over a complex sequence of

copying and recopying by using a contact printer equipped with register pins. Punch register holes in each new sheet of film or paper.

● **The cheapest punch** register system is a good-quality office punch inlaid into a wooden board to allow the film to slide level into the jaws of the punch. Make register pins with wooden dowelling rod. These can be taped to a bar for use under the enlarger or used in a contact printer.

● **Photographic punch register** systems such as Kodak's ensure greater precision than possible with a home-made system.

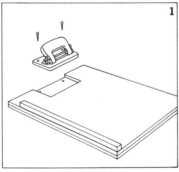

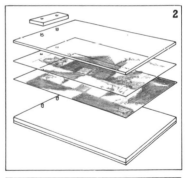

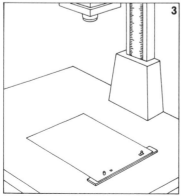

1. Home-made registration board
2. Registered contact print
3. Registering separations under the enlarger
4. Kodak punch system

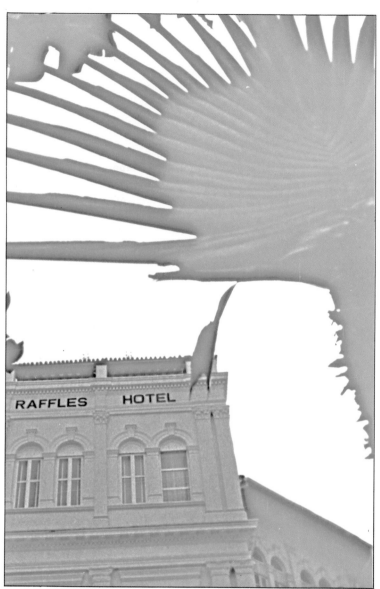

▲ Many of the more spectacular darkroom effects depend on working in register. This colorful view of the Raffles Hotel in Singapore was created by first printing the original slide onto neg/pos paper to give an image reversed in both tone and color. I then punched this print and a second sheet of unexposed paper with register holes and laid them in a contact printer in complete darkness. I switched on the enlarger to expose the second sheet — since the exposure was through paper, the exposure needed to be 20 times as long as normal. I then sandwiched both prints in register and contact printed onto a third sheet.

MAKE COLOR SEPARATIONS

Color separation is an essential feature of many advanced darkroom manipulations, and it is worth spending some time learning the technique. Color separation involves splitting the color image into its blue, green and red components by making three copies on black and white film through blue, green and red filters respectively.

● **Start with any original** —
artwork, flat copy, color slide,
color negative. But if you start with
a color negative make a normal
print and work from this.

● **Work from a color slide** if you
can; it is much easier. Photograph
artwork and flat copy on slide film
if necessary.

● **Include a gray scale** in the
picture if you take it specifically

for color separation. It will make
exposure calculation and color
balance much easier.

● **Use panchromatic b&w film** for
the separations. This means
working in total darkness at times,
for there is no safelight for
panchromatic films, but it must be
panchromatic to record tones for
all the colors of the original. On
orthochromatic film, reds would
not be recorded.

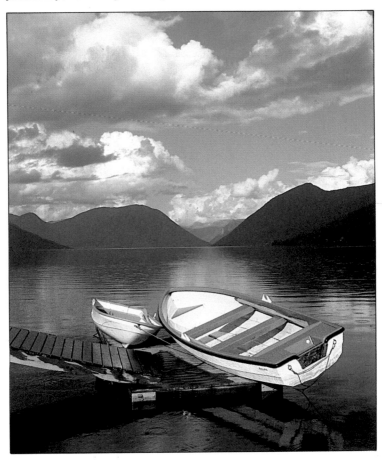

● **Work with sheet film** — 5 × 4in is ideal — unless you specifically want 35mm copies. Separations on sheet film are easier to work with.

● **Use narrow cut filters** to ensure complete separation. An ideal separation set is the Wratten filters 29, 61 and 47B.

● **Make separations on sheet film** by projecting the slide in the enlarger in exactly the same way as for ordinary prints.

● **Register each sheet** using a register bar taped to the enlarger baseboard (page 116).

● **Cut the corners** to help identify each separation.

● **Start exposure tests** for each negative with the following exposures if you are using the Wratten filter set suggested and enlarging 35mm originals onto 5 × 4. With the lens set at $f8$, expose through the blue filter for 25 seconds, the green for 15 seconds and the red for 30.

● **Process the separations** in trays as recommended. Develop all three negatives together, but leave the red and green separations in for 4½ minutes and the blue for 7 for uniform contrast.

▼ Separations from color slides give three separation negatives. If you need positives, simply contactprint on sheet film.

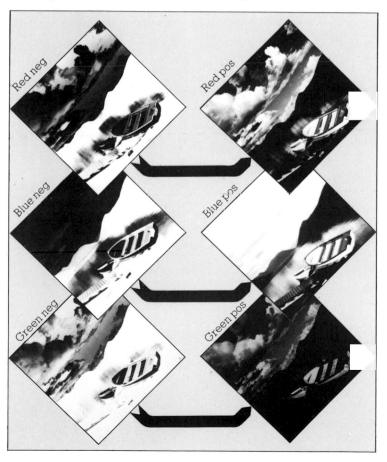

POSTERIZE PRINTS

With a technique called posterization you can create a print in bold striking colors, like a poster, from any original, whether color or black and white. It involves making a series of tone separations on black and white film, then printing them in register through color filters onto color print paper in any combination you wish. The result depends entirely on the filters chosen.

● **Copy color originals** onto ordinary b&w film. B&w negatives can be used directly.

● **Make tone separations** from the b&w copy or original by printing onto three sheets of lith film, exposing one print normally, underexposing one by 1½ stops and overexposing the third by 1½ stops.

● **Choose the size** of the lith film sheets according to the size of

print you want, unless you have an enlarger capable of printing from large sheets of film.

● **Ensure perfect register** by taping a peg-bar onto the enlarger baseboard and punching register holes in each sheet of film. For register techniques see p. 116.

● **Contact print** each separation onto lith film again so that you have three negative and three positive separations.

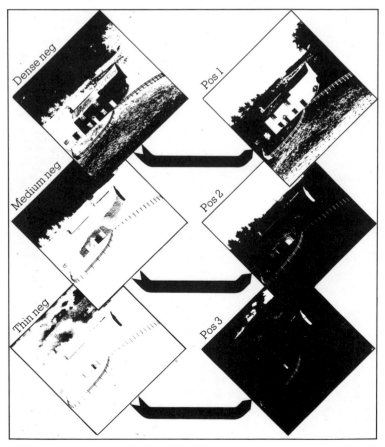

● **Number each separation** so that you can repeat the print.

● **Make a posterized print** by contact printing (or enlarging) the separations onto b&w or color print paper.

● **For b&w posterizations,** simply print all three separations in sequence onto b&w paper, giving only enough exposure to each separation to produce a mid-gray tone in the shadows.

● **For simple color** posterizations, expose a single separation onto color print paper with a colored light source.

● **For multi-colored** posterizations print various combinations of separations onto color print paper, using a different color light for each exposure.

● **Color the light** by placing different colored filters under the enlarger or in the enlarger filter drawer.

▼ The posterized image of the house began with three tone separations of varying density made from the original transparency by contact printing onto high contrast lith film. These were contacted back to positives and then printed down in combination, using different light sources.

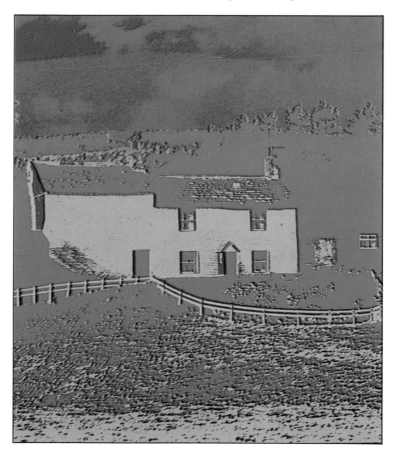

USE EQUIDENSITY FILM

Darkroom techniques that alter the image are becoming more advanced, partly due to the progress made with specialised films for scientific purposes, such as the unique Agfacontour high-contrast equidensity film. These new materials encourage photographers and graphic designers to exploit their remarkable characteristics and properties of extreme contrast, creating effects of broad, rich posterization, and pictures that seem to shimmer with light. You can have great fun experimenting with the unusual behaviour of these emulsions, using your own shots and transforming originals into arresting color images.

● **Produce an equidensity image** by copying your original onto Agfacontour film. Agfacontour reproduces highlights and shadows in black, but in between these areas, there is a thin, clear line joining points of equal tone density. The effect is to produce an outline of each tonal area in the picture — almost like a drawing.

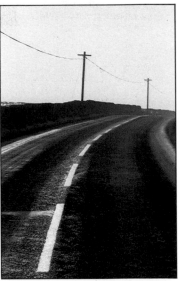

● **Contact print** your original negative onto a sheet of lith film to make a positive. Recopy the lith to make a lith negative.

● **Expose a sheet** of Agfacontour film in contact with the lith negative. Establish an exposure test in steps of 10, 20, 40, and 80 seconds at f8.

● **Develop the film** in Agfacontour developer for 2 minutes at 20°C, then in a 3 percent acetic acid bath for 30 seconds. Fix as normal and wash for 15 minutes. This gives you a 'first order' Agfacontour image.

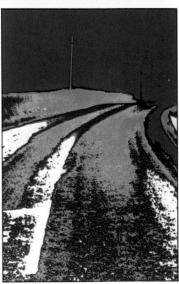

● **Assess the exposure** by examining the processed sheet in normal light. Equidensity lines will not form if exposure is too great or too small. An underexposed sheet is bluish black in color; an overexposed sheet is brownish black.

● **Make a lith film contact** with your first order image. Use the same exposure and processing to obtain the 'second order' image. Continue with this sequence to establish your 'third order' image with three equidensity lines.

● **Print through three** color filters in turn to get the final color image.

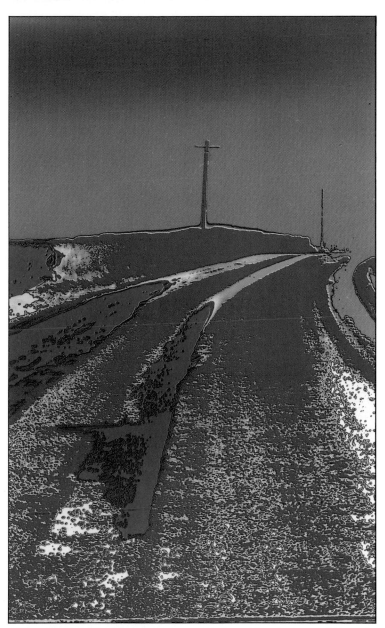

▲ The startling color pictures above and opposite (top), were made from a low-contrast black and white negative from an original shot, opposite. This was exposed onto equidensity Agfacontour film. A second and a third equidensity image followed and the three final images, each with a differing line effect, were printed in turn through color filters. The final result depends on the filtration and the number of equidensity negatives used.

MASK FOR CONTRAST

Contrast masking is a technique for increasing or reducing contrast, especially in slides, with a degree of accuracy impossible with dodging and burning-in masks. But it is also an interesting way of producing false color images. The technique involves printing the original in contact with a thin, underexposed black and white copy onto color reversal paper.

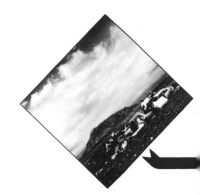

● **Decide** whether you want a sharp mask or an unsharp mask. Both are produced the same way — by making a contact from the original — but an unsharp mask is made by separating the two emulsions with a diffusing sheet. The unsharp mask is more usual and ensures that slight errors of registration are not noticeable.

To reduce contrast
● **Make an unsharp mask** by exposing special masking film or, if that is impossible, ordinary b&w film in contact with the original.

● **Experiment with exposure** and development until you have a very thin, flat negative with little or no image in the highlight areas.

To increase contrast
● **Use separation negative film** to make a sharp (emulsion to emulsion) internegative from the original slide.

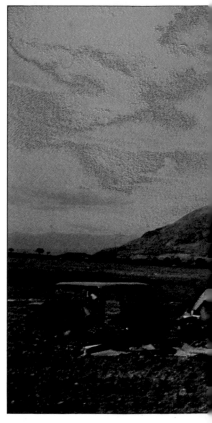

● **Experiment with exposure** and development until you have a crisp, detailed image.

● **Sandwich the interneg** with another piece of the same film in register and give a short exposure to produce an underexposed image with no detail in the highlights.

To print with masks
● **Sandwich the mask** you need in register with the original. When printing, increase exposure to allow for the density of the mask.

To alter color
● **Sandwich** the color negative or transparency with a negative or positive contrast mask and expose with a colored light source. Or use both masks, and a double exposure.

▼ The two contrast masks below were used in a double exposure to make the picture of a car cemetery. The first exposure was for the original transparency sandwiched with an underexposed contrast mask; the second for the transparency sandwiched with the positive of the mask. By using different color light sources for each exposure, the division between highlights and the rest of the image was enhanced.

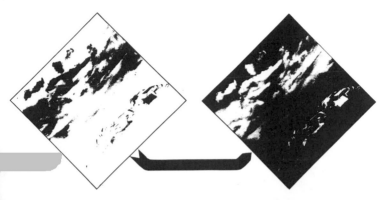

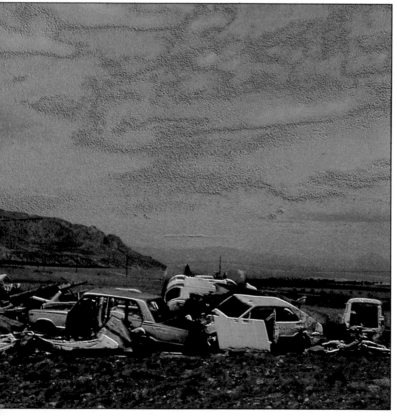

STRIP IN IMAGES

Stripping-in is an effective way of combining several different images in a single print. The effects are similar to montage, but the various elements of the picture are not physically cut out and stuck down in position. Instead, they are cut out photographically using combinations of positive and negative masks and then assembled by a multiple exposure. Strip-ins are usually made in a copy camera, but they can be done just as effectively with an enlarger, provided you are careful to ensure perfect registration. Follow the principles already demonstrated in this section.

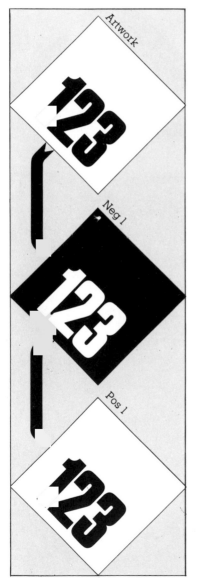

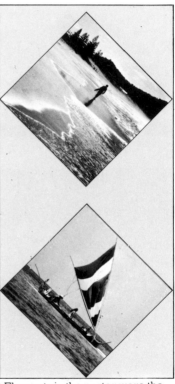

▲ Elements in the poster were the figures 123 on a b&w print and two color transparencies. The 123 image was copied in the enlarger onto high contrast 35mm film. The resulting negative was printed onto a registered-punched sheet of lith film to make the positive mask. The negative mask was then made by contact printing the positive onto lith film. To strip in each color image, the beach transparency was printed onto pos/pos color paper through the positive mask. Then the sailboat was printed through the 123 negative in reverse and in register.

● **Size each element** by making a tracing of the final picture.

● **Establish exposures** and filtration with test strips in the normal way.

● **Make positive** and negative masks by copying a simple shape or image onto lith film.

● **Remember to register** the images carefully by laying them up on punched cells.

● **Expose the images** onto the same print through the appropriate mask.

● **Enlarge the strip-in** by copying.

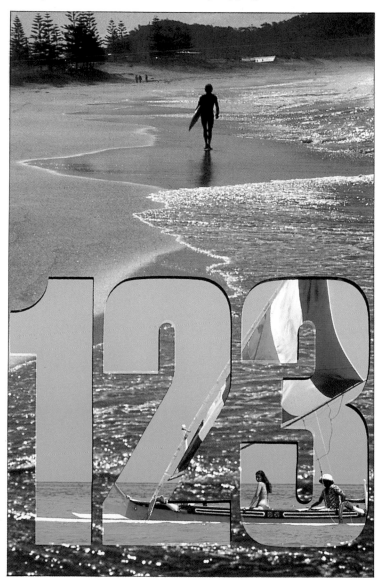

CREATE A MANDALA

A mandala is a motif arranged in the form of a repeated pattern, rather like a Rorsach inkblot or the mirror-image of a kaleidoscope. Photographic mandalas can have graphic design applications for wallpapers and textiles and you can make powerful and intriguing mandalas by such techniques as photomontage, multiple printing or — as in the example below — by combining duplicate slides.

● **Choose an image** of a regular, uniform shape that lends itself well to repetition. For a color mandala, photograph it on slide film. For a black and white mandala make a contact positive.

● **Shoot an existing object,** an abstract detail against a plain background for example, or a greatly magnified fragment shot with a macro lens. The mandala here was based on a crankshaft.

● **Look through** your stock shots to find a suitable image. Pictures with bold diagonals and converging lines and broad, simple shapes are ideal.

● **Isolate sections** of posterized, solarized and prism-filter images. Don't overlook your black and white prints. High-contrast images, silhouettes, and pictures shot on lith film make strong patterns and motifs of considerable impact.

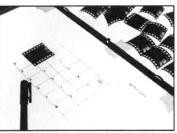

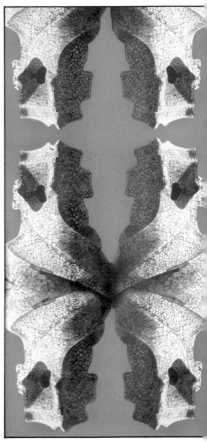

▸ The mandala on the right was made with 18 duplicates of the original slide on Kodak 5071 copying film. After making the duplicates, I drew up a grid on tracing paper using a slide to determine the size of the grid squares and taped this over a lightbox (above). I then carefully cut away the borders of the slides, using a sharp scalpel and a metal straight-edge. With a fine brush, I placed a bare minimum of glue along the edge of each slide and stuck the slides together over the grid, waiting for the glue to set on each join before adding the next slide.

● **Make a series of copies** of your original, some with the image the right way round, some with the image reversed.

● **Reverse the image** simply by 'flopping' the film over and exposing through the front.

● **Make duplicate slides** if you want to make a series of copies of your finished mandala. Sticking slides together accurately requires considerable skill, but you will be able to use the finished mandala to make any number of copies by contact printing. Copies on 35mm film may also be relatively cheap to make.

● **Copy onto 5×4 film** if you only want a few images in your mandala. This will be more expensive, but the large slides are much easier to work with and give a bigger print.

● **Join slides** by drawing a grid for the images on tracing paper, taping this to a lightbox and laying the slides on this. Trim the slides to mate exactly with a scalpel and a metal rule, and stick them together by lightly brushing the film edges with clear adhesive, making sure the slides do not stick to the paper.

● **Montage prints of the original** if you feel joining slides is too tricky, then photograph the result. Or make a series of exposures onto the same sheet of paper, using masks and a pre-drawn grid to establish positions.

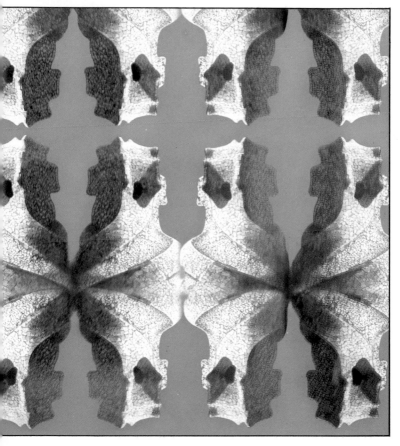

EXPLOIT NEONS

Opal materials are commonly used to provide an even light source for viewing and projecting film. But you can also use them to create spectacular haloes like neon lights around an image. The effect, called neoning, depends on the way opal film scatters light and works in the same way as the corona in a total eclipse. The idea is to make a negative silhouette and a positive. The neon is then created by sandwiching a sheet of opal film and plate glass between the negative and positive and illuminating the negative from behind. Without the opal, the positive silhouette would block all light coming through the negative mask. With the opal, just enough light is scattered to create a brilliant outline.

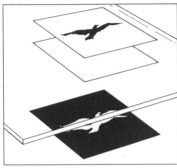

▲ I created the image below by photographing the lith positive against a blue light then taping the negative underneath opal film and glass and illuminating it with yellow light to create a neon for a second exposure.

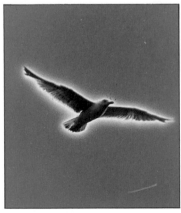

▶ For this picture I made three flash exposures of a gymnast, copied the negatives onto lith film, and contacted the copies onto lith to make negative and positive masks. Using a green light, I shot a neon of each on the same frame.

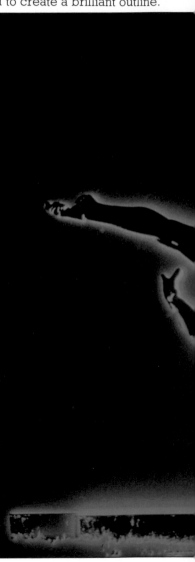

● **Use any original,** providing it has a strong, simple outline.

● **Copy onto lith film** to create a negative mask. Retouch to enhance the silhouette.

● **Contact print the lith copy** onto lith to make the positive.

● **Tape the negative** to thick plate glass.

● **Tape the opal film** to the other side of the glass. Use tracing paper if you have no opal film.

● **Register the positive** carefully over the negative and tape down.

● **Illuminate the negative** from underneath. Color the light with filters if you wish.

● **Photograph from above.**

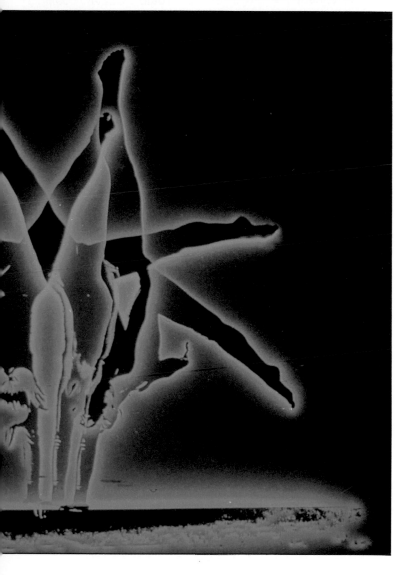

PRINT BY DYE TRANSFER 1

For sheer quality, there is little to beat the dye transfer process. In the hands of a skilled practitioner, it can give color prints of matchless quality that will long outlive color prints made by conventional methods. The technique is undoubtedly complex and requires considerable patience, and the materials are costly. But once mastered, the richness of the colors, and the almost total control, are ample reward for the enormous effort. The process entails making three color separations from a color original and printing these onto special matrix film which gives a relief image in gelatin. Each of the three matrices is dyed a different color and the dye is transferred to a specially-prepared paper base by printing all three precisely in register.

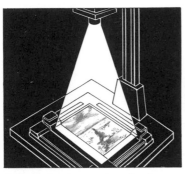

1 To make the matrices for dye transfer, you need three separation negatives of the original. Under a red safelight, print each of the negatives in turn onto matrix film to make three positive matrices. Test for exposure as described opposite.

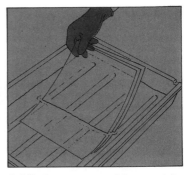

2 Mix the two parts of the special tanning developer energetically, pour into the first tray and immediately immerse all three exposed matrices in turn. Agitate continuously for all the two minute development to keep the matrices apart.

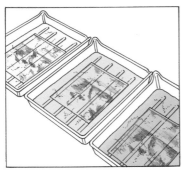

4 Start the laying down process by soaking the three matrices in hand-hot water for four minutes. Transfer the matrices to their respective dye baths and leave for five minutes at room temperature, agitating frequently to ensure even dye uptake.

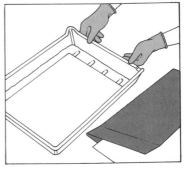

5 Condition the receiving paper for 20 minutes in the bath supplied. Remove the cyan matrix from its dye bath and drain until the dye forms droplets. Immerse in 1% acetic acid bath for 1 minute, drain and transfer to second acid bath. Prepare to print.

What you need
Normal darkroom items plus:
equipment for making color
separations (see pages 118-19);
gray step tablet; exposure meter;
matrix film and chemicals
(including two-part developer and
dyes); receiving paper and
conditioner; laying down slab; at
least seven large developing rays
for all the solutions; register punch
and peg system; lightbox; masking
tape; roller squeegee.

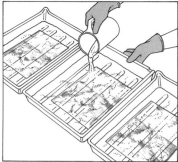

3 Transfer to a water rinse for 30
seconds and then into non-
hardening fixer for five minutes.
Then place each matrice in a
different tray of hand-hot water to
dissolve the unexposed gelatin.
When clear, quench in cold water,
dry and make registration holes.

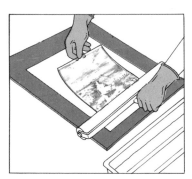

6 Position the receiving paper
on the laying down board. With
the cyan matrix relief side down
over the register pins without
touching the paper. Then roll the
matrix onto the paper out from
the pins. Repeat the process for
the magenta and yellow matrices.

● **Make separation negatives**
either in the darkroom (see
pages 118-19) or by making three
exposures in the camera through
the appropriate red, green and
blue filters. Accurate
registration is easier if you work
in the darkroom. To get
separation negatives from color
negatives, you must make
positives and copy these.

● **Color negatives** can be
separated directly onto special
panchromatic matrix film through
the three separation filters. But this
means working in total darkness.

● **Test for exposure** with the cyan
separation when making the
matrices. Use an exposure meter
if you can. Otherwise, make a
normal printing test strip but lay a
paper clip on the matrix film as
each band is exposed.

● **Judge test exposures** by looking
for the band in which highlights
are just clear of tone and gelatin.
With the paper clip, look for the
band which just gives enough
exposure to create a relief image
of the clip by a faint raised line.

● **Develop the matrices at 68°F**
(20°C), ideally by keeping the
room at this temperature.

● **Agitate** by pulling the bottom
matrix out and placing it on the top
of the pile every 15 seconds.

● **Make register holes** in each
matrix in the following manner.
Tape the cyan matrix, relief-side
down, on a lightbox in a register
punch. Carefully align the
magenta matrix by eye using a
magnifier. Punch register holes
through the cyan and magenta
matrices. Repeat the procedure
with the yellow matrix, registering
it over the cyan matrix.

● **Lay the print down** on heavy
plate glass set in a wooden frame
to accommodate register pins.

● **Print the matrices** in the order
cyan, magenta, yellow, leaving
each in place for five minutes.

PRINT BY DYE TRANSFER 2

Once you have mastered the basics of dye transfer, you can use it as a starting point for a whole range of derivations and effects. Some of the effects can be subtle and surprising like the baffling change in the color of the car opposite; some are as startling and colorful as posterizations. The key to these effects lies in exploiting the matrices.

● **Dye the matrices** in the wrong colors — the cyan matrix in magenta dye, and so on. But always lay down the darkest, cyan matrix first.

● **Try new dyes** for the coloring the matrices.

● **Don't use more than three** colors on any single print.

● **Make the matrices** from separations on lith film.

● **Make matrices from any original** — color slide, negative, positive, black and white, anything.

● **Overprint the matrices** on black and white prints.

● **Combine negative matrices** with positives.

● **Combine images** by laying down the matrices from different pictures.

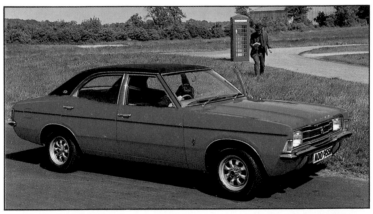

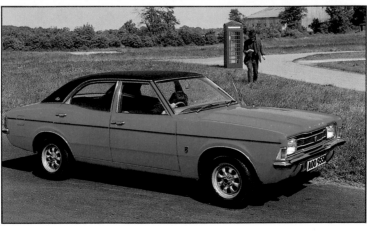

▼ Dye transfer prints make an ideal base for retouching, because the paper and dyes can be matched closely to the airbrushing dyes. The straight image of the man on the sofa (right) was used to make a dye transfer print and on this the shaded area was introduced by retouching to give the impression that a picture once hung there. I also applied the matrices to the print a second time to increase contrast. For this second transfer I left each matrix in its dye bath for 20 seconds, not the full five minutes.

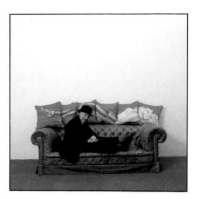

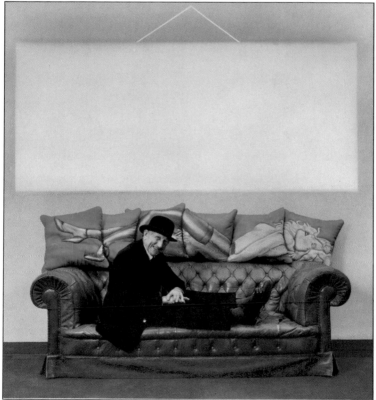

◄ I printed both these images from the same image by dye transfer. The red car was a straight print made in the way described previously (page 132-3). To turn the car blue, I made a new set of matrices from the original separation negatives sandwich with a mask of the car body. A print from these matrices yielded a straight image of the background. I then re-exposed the red-filter separation negatives, sandwiched with a reverse mask of the car body to give a matrix suitable for printing the car body in any color I cared to dye the matrix — in this case blue.

MOUNT YOUR PRINTS

Your favourite shots deserve to be properly displayed, and you owe it to yourself to see that the prints are shown off to their best advantage, whether in your home or at an exhibition of photographs. Make sure your prints are spotless and carefully retouched where necessary. It isn't essential to frame your pictures, but mounts and supports should be thick enough to prevent prints from warping and buckling. Cut-out mounts, preferably of a neutral tone or plain white, will considerably enhance even your best shots, and although thick mounting board is expensive, the investment will be worthwhile. You can buy ready-cut mounts, with matching glass and clips. DIY kit frames are also available in a wide range of standard sizes.

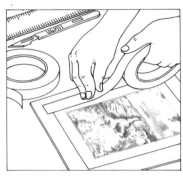

1 Use a pencil to mark where your print is to be placed on the mounting board. Leave space for the borders. Align the print and tape it to the board either by taping the underside and the print and peeling away the release paper.

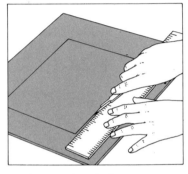

2 Measure the window area on your covering mounting board according to the size of your print and mark the rectangle lightly with a pencil. Cut out with a sharp scalpel, slanting to cut a bevel. Watch that you don't overrun the corners. Erase pencil marks.

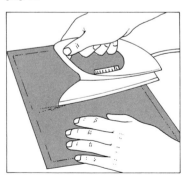

1 Alternatively, place the print face down and lay the tissue over the back. Gently tack down with the tip of a domestic iron on a low setting. If it fails to melt the glue, increase the heat. Start in the middle and work out, but don't tack the corners.

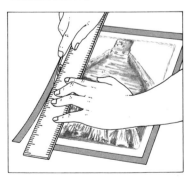

2 Now turn the print over and trim away any surplus tissue, or trim both print and tissue together, with a sharp knife. The edges must be flush to avoid the tissue appearing around the outside of the print, unless you intend to cover it with a window mount.

● **Cutting a mount.** The borders of a mount should be of a generous width, the bottom border deeper than the top and sides. With thick card, cut the window mount on a bevel and to the same overall dimensions as the border.

● **Wet and Dry mounting.** The simplest technique is to use an adhesive such as latex, applied with a spreader, or an aerosol of spray adhesive.

● **Alternatives include** double-sided adhesive film, where you pull off a back and front release paper, and dry mounting tissue, perhaps the most effective way.

● **The tissue is impregnated** with glue which melts when ironed to form a firm bond between print and mount. You can use a domestic flat iron as described below.

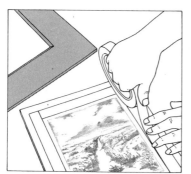

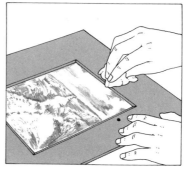

3 Use double-sided tape along the edges of the print to sandwich the two boards together. Excess rebate on the window mount can be trimmed away with the knife. If you intend to frame your picture, check that the frame section will accept two boards plus glass.

4 Remove the release paper on the tape, align the two mounting boards and press firmly together. Use a cloth to avoid leaving finger marks on the mount. A firmer bond between print and support can be made with dry-mounting tissue.

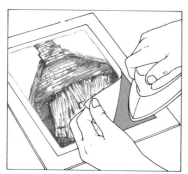

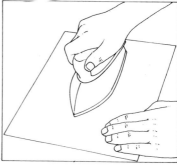

3 Position the print on the supporting mount, and square to the edges, having marked the position with a pencil and ruler. Keep the print in position while you lift each corner in turn, and tack the tissue to the board with the iron.

4 You now need to protect the face of your print with smooth, unwaxed paper. Heavy brown wrapping paper is ideal. Adjust the iron to a low setting and apply firm pressure to the print, working outwards from the center. Check that the tissue is bonding.

STORE FILM IMAGES

No photographic images last forever. Color photographs in particular are prone to fading. But you can extend their life considerably by storing them under the right conditions. Proper, organized storage will also help you to find the image you want with the minimum of fuss. This, in turn, further helps to preserve your pictures, for nothing reduces the life of film images more than handling.

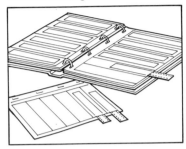

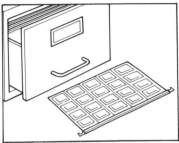

● **Store all films** in dry conditions. Any dampness in the air will be taken up by the film very rapidly, softening the emulsion and laying it open to attack.

● **Include a bag** of silica gel in your storage cabinet or bag to absorb any moisture in the atmosphere, particularly when storing color film.

● **Avoid dust and grit** like the plague. Make sure your storage cabinet is free from dust and clean film prior to storage with an antistatic brush.

● **Keep the film cool.** Film will last virtually forever in a dry refrigerator.

● **Store film in darkness.** Color film fades rapidly in bright light, particularly sunlight and fluorescent light.

● **Never handle films** more than necessary. Refer to the contact sheets or duplicates if you can.

● **Store negatives** on negative file sheets that hold six or seven strips of negatives and can be filed neatly away in a ring-binder.
● **Store slides** in clear plastic display sleeves if you have only a small collection, or use them for your most cherished or most used slides. They are expensive,

▲ Negative file sheets are a neat way of storing negatives. Slide display sleeves, often known as 'viewpacks', are a convenient and attractive way of storing slides.

but protect each slide in its own individual pocket and allow you to view up to 24 slides at a time without ever touching them. Some versions file neatly into ring-binders, some file into the rack draw of a filing cabinet. As with negatives, you should use polythene, not PVC, sleeves.

● **Store** large slide collections in specially-designed storage boxes with slots for individual slides.

● **Store** complete slide shows in magazines ready to load straight into the projector. Bear in mind that magazines for some projectors can be very expensive.

● **Use paper file sheets** if you rarely need to look at the negatives. Special acid-free paper does not react with the film.

● **Use clear plastic sheets** if you need to look at the negatives often. You can see the images clearly without removing the film from its sleeve. But bear in mind that some clear plastics give off vapors that may attack the film if you use clear plastic sleeves; use polythene sleeves instead.

PROJECT SLIDES

Unlike prints which can be handed round for viewing or displayed prominently on a wall, slides can only be seen properly by projection. Yet photographers who put considerable effort into getting high-quality slides will often undermine the value of their work by casual slide projection. To show your slides off to best effect, you should put as much care into projection as any other stage.

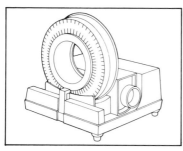 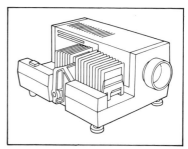

● **Black out the room** as well as you can. Any light leaks will make the richest colors seem pale and washed out. The brightness of the slide projector light will not compensate for a bright room.

● **Black out the projector** as well. Light often spills from the ventilator slats and it is worth holding a sheet of black card or a piece of black velvet between the top of the projector and the screen.

● **Choose your screen** with care. A wall painted plain matt white is quite satisfactory, but a proper screen is better.

● **Beaded screens** give a very bright, clear image, but can only be seen over a very narrow angle.

● **Position the screen** facing away from any potential light leaks — that is, up against the window rather than facing it.

● **Set up the projector** level with the middle of the screen.

● **Raise the projector** to the right height on a purpose-built stand. If you improvize, make sure the stand is rigid. A pair of step ladders makes a good base; a pile of telephone directories on the edge of a table does not.

● **Project** through a serving hatch

if you can. This will keep a noisy projector out of ear shot. You can change the slides with a remote control switch if you have one.

● **Don't tilt the projector** to gain height. This will distort the image — the top will be bigger than the bottom, an effect called 'keystoning'.

● **Choose the focal length** of your enlarger to suit the size of room you have and the size of image you want. Bear in mind that you need a very powerful projector to project large images well.

● **Tape down trailing wires.**

● **Keep a spare bulb handy** — bulbs can blow at the most awkward times.

● **Carefully align** all the slides to be shown so that they can be slotted quickly into the projector or the magazine the right way round. Remember, slides are projected upside down with the emulsion facing the screen.

● **Stick spots** on the bottom lefthand corner of each slide to help alignment. This goes at the top righthand corner when you feed the slide into the projector.

● **Don't mix** dense and thin slides or different types of film.

MAKE A SLIDE SHOW

Casually projecting a loosely organized collection of holiday pictures is simple and straightforward. But you may sometimes want to attempt something a little more structured. You may even want to provide an informative commentary, rather than off the cuff remarks. Whatever your motive, you will find the results of organizing your slides into a proper show rewarding. By editing and trimming the sequence of images, you will find that their effect is far more concise and powerful. The weak pictures that often dilute the effect of a slide session should be discarded ruthlessly and the better pictures should be used only if they contribute to the overall effect. You may find this leaves you with very few slides, but this is not such a bad thing.

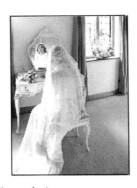

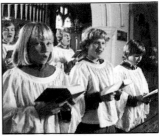

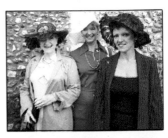

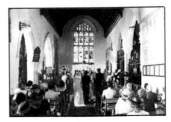

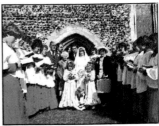

▲ A wedding is an obvious candidate for a slide show and benefits enormously from a narrative approach. Try to think about how the slides will build up into a show as you shoot and pick your shots accordingly. Follow the celebrations through from beginning to end, with shots to illustrate each step on the way. A shot of the bride getting ready at home makes an obvious opening shot. Further shots show the guests arriving at the church, the choir singing, the entry of the bride, and the ceremony itself. Then there are the traditional shots of the wedding party outside the church. The strong vertical frame of the church door makes an ideal transition from the horizontal to vertical formats. The tall couple make a similarly effective transition back to horizontal as they leave the church. Further shots show the highlights of the reception. And a shot of guests waving off the happy couple makes a neat finish.

● **Use perfect slides.** Reject any that are blurred, poorly exposed or in anyway substandard.

● **Try to keep** the same format, vertical or horizontal. If you need to switch, look for an image with a strong rectangular shape to make the transition. A doorway is ideal.

● **Keep movement** in the slide, such as cars, in the same direction.

● **Make a narrative** to give the show a structure. Follow an event right through from beginning to end.

● **Aim for variety** of scale and subject. Mix long shots with close-ups and people with places.

● **Look for scene-setting shots,** such as road-signs, overall views and so on, which you can slot in to introduce a sequence.

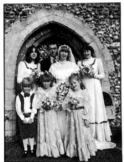

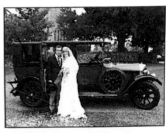

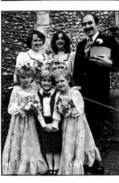

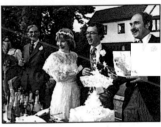

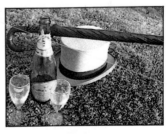

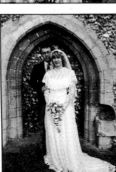

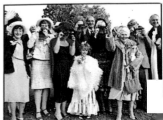

EXPOSURE COMPENSATION

Printing exposure varies not only between individual negatives, but also for the same negative when you alter the enlarging lens aperture, the magnification or the filtration. However, there is no need to make a new test strip for each change. Simply consult the tables below

Changes in print size

	Original exposure time (seconds)						
	1	2	4	8	16	20	30
Magnification	New exposure time (seconds)						
2x	2	5½	11	22	44	55	80
2.25x	2½	6½	13	26	55	65	95
2.5x	3	8	16	32	65	80	120
2.75x	3½	9½	18	37	75	95	140
3x	4	11	22	45	90	110	165
3.5x	5¼	15	30	60	120	150	220
4x	7	18	38	76	150	200	280
5x	11	30	60	120	240	300	450
6x	16	45	90	180	360	450	—
8x	30	80	160	320	—	—	—
10x	50	130	270	—	—	—	—

To find the extra exposure needed for a larger print from a negative, you must work out how many times bigger the new print will be than your original reference print. To do this, simply measure the length of one side in both the original print and the new print. Divide one into the other to find the magnification. Then consult the table above for the new exposure time. The blank spaces in the table indicate that the new exposure would be so long that 'reciprocity failure' may become a severe prob! m. It is better not to make giant enlargements from negatives so dense, but if you must, open the aperture to keep the exposure as short as possible and make a test strip. With color, you may need to alter the filtration.

Changes in filtration

	Filter factors					
	Yellow		Magenta		Cyan	
Filter strength	Kodak	Agfa	Kodak	Agfa	Kodak	Agfa
05	1.1	1.1	1.2	1.2	1.1	1.2
10	1.1	1.1	1.3	1.2	1.2	1.2
20	1.1	1.2	1.5	1.2	1.3	1.3
30	1.1	1.2	1.7	1.3	1.4	1.4
40	1.1	1.2	1.9	1.4	1.5	1.5
50	1.1	1.2	2.1	1.5	1.6	1.7

To find the exposure change needed when changing filtration, consult the table to find the filter factor for each new filter added or subtracted. When adding filters, multiply the original exposure by the filter factor to find the new exposure. When subtracting filters, divide by the filter factor. When changing two colors, multiply (or divide) the original exposure time first by the factor for one color, then by the factor for the other.

CONVERSIONS

Although there have been strenuous efforts in recent years to standardize measures, many makers of darkroom materials still persist in using their own preferred system. So some instructions may call for measurements in fluid ounces, others in cubic centilitres, and so on. To avoid confusion, it is worth trying to standardize your own measuring system to your own standard for every process you use. These tables provide some of the most commonly used conversions.

Conversion factors

To convert measurements in one system to measurements in another, simply multiply by the conversion factor given here.

Length

| inches to cm | 2.54 | cm to inches | 0.3937 |
| feet to m | 0.3048 | m to feet | 3.2808 |

Volume

| US fluid oz to ml | 29.57 | ml to US fluid oz | 0.0338 |
| UK fluid oz to ml | 28.41 | ml to UK fluid oz | 0.0352 |

Weight

| ounces to g | 28.35 | g to ounces | 0.0353 |
| pounds to kg | 0.4536 | kg to pounds | 2.2047 |

Temperatures
Temperatures may be given either in degrees Fahrenheit (F) or Centigrade (C) on the Celsius scale. To convert temperatures in one scale to temperatures in the other, use the formula given opposite.

Fahrenheit to Centigrade:
degrees $C = (\text{degrees } F - 32) \times 5/9$

Centigrade to Fahrenheit:
degrees $F = (\text{degrees } C \times 9/5) + 32$

Fahrenheit to Centigrade

°F	°C	°F	°C
50	10.0	75	23.89
55	12.78	80	26.67
60	15.56	85	29.44
65	18.33	90	32.22
67	19.44	95	35.00
68	20.00	100	37.78
69	20.55	101	38.34
70	21.11	105	40.56

Centigrade to Fahrenheit

°C	°F	°C
10	50.0	30
15	59.0	3〔
19	66.2	
20	68.0	
21	69.9	
24	75.2	
26	78.8	
28	82.4	

FAULTS IN FILM PROCESSING

Defects that can appear in all types of films are listed under the 'black and white' heading. Faults specific to color negative or transparency films are listed under the appropriate headings. Unless otherwise stated, faults in processed film cannot be rectified, and the remedies described refer to future processing technique.

Black and white film

● Scratches along film length
Cause: Grit dragged in contact with film, when it is being either wound out of or rewound into film cassette; grit dragged along film when it is being passed through fingers or squeegeed prior to drying; possible rough spot on film pressure plate in camera (rare).
Remedy: Protect film cassettes from dust, grit and sand — don't unwrap film or open package until film is to be loaded in camera. With reloadable cassettes, check that felt light trap is clean. Ensure squeegee is clean before using and/or use lighter pressure.

● Isolated light or clear areas on negatives
Cause: Air bubbles have stuck to film during processing.
Remedy: Tap the developing tank after agitation to dislodge air bubbles.

● Dark streaks and/or blobs of irregular shape
Cause: A light leak has locally fogged the film before it was developed.
Remedy: Prevent by checking reusable film cassettes and light-tightness of darkroom and developing tank. Ensure that a gasket is used between the developing tank and its lid and that the tank has no hairline cracks.

● Clear or light band along edge 'm
· Insufficient solution in ing tank to completely film.
llow the tank nsure that is used for the at of films heck using

● Negatives too dense and contrast too high
Cause: The development temperature was too high, or the developing time too long, or the agitation during development was excessive.
Remedy: Farmer's reducer can make thick negatives somewhat thinner. In future, check the developer directions for the correct time, temperature and agitation for the particular film being processed and control the temperature of the solution by placing it in a water bath constantly adjusted to the correct temperature. If this is impossible, adjust the developing time to the temperature actually used.

● Negatives too thin but contrast near normal
Cause: The development temperature was too low, or the development time too short, or the agitation during development was insufficient.
Remedy: Control the development process as described above.

● Milky white appearance
Cause: Insufficient fixing bath time, exhausted fixer or incorrect fixer concentration.
Remedy: Try refixing in new solution; check manufacturer's recommendations concerning dilution and the amount of use. Mark your reusable fixer solution bottle with date of mixing, concentration and the number of films that one batch will treat.

● Overall crazed pattern ('reticulation')
Cause: The 'shock' of inconsistent solution temperatures — for example, warm developer and cold fixer.
Remedy: Ensure that all solutions and the water wash are at the same temperature.

● **Film completely clear**
Cause: Film accidentally placed in fixer instead of developer.
Remedy: None for affected films.

Color negative film

● **Negatives too dense and contrasty**
Cause: Overdevelopment; on Agfa film, if the orange mask is also too dense, then the likely cause is excessive bleaching.
Remedy: Follow the manufacturer's directions on time and temperature carefully. Avoid excessive tank draining times.

● **Negatives too contrasty, density normal**
Cause: Excessive bleaching.
Remedy: Check maker's directions regarding bleaching time, temperature and dilution.

● **Spots** in which the orange mask can be seen but no image, or only a faint one
Cause: Air bubbles stuck to film during processing.
Remedy: Tap the tank after agitation.

● **Irregularly shaped streaks** running downwards from the film's sprocket holes
Cause: Developer was caught in holes during excessive draining time.
Remedy: Start to drain slightly before that stage is completed, and progress quickly to the next stage.

● **Overall purple cast** with a dense image
Cause: Fogging.
Remedy: Check the light-tightness of the developing tank and of the darkroom itself.

Color slide film

● **Light-colored streaks** or irregular spots, often yellowish
Cause: Fogging.
Remedy: Check the light-tightness of the developing tank and the darkroom.

● **Dark spots,** possibly with a reddish cast
Cause: Air bubbles sticking to the film during development.
Remedy: After agitation, tap the tank bottom sharply.

● **Film too dense and dark, with a reddish cast**
Cause: Underdevelopment.
Remedy: Use fresh chemicals. Mark the quantity for which a batch can be used on the bottle. Check the directions for proper time, temperature and dilution.

● **Too blue, with smoky blacks**
Cause: Reversal bath (if the film was chemically reversed) was too concentrated; or the color developer was too weak; or the first developer was contaminated.
Remedy: Carefully label bottles and always use the same bottles for the same solutions. Check the directions for the correct dilutions.

● **Green cast, with smoky blacks**
Cause: Reversal procedure was omitted or inadequate; or film was outdated or badly stored.
Remedy: Check that fresh solutions are being used. Check time, temperature and agitation for the reversal procedure (if chemical), or check lamp wattage and film-to-lamp distance against the directions.

● **Too light, with a blue cast**
Cause: Color developer possibly contaminated with first developer.
Remedy: Label bottles correctly and always use the same bottles for the same solutions.

● **Milky, cloudy appearance**
Cause: Inadequate fixing time, incorrect fixer concentration, fixer exhausted or too cold.
Remedy: Refix in fresh solution.

● **Highlight areas appear pink**
Cause: Insufficient wash following the color development stage.
Remedy: Follow directions.

● **Yellow-brown staining**
Cause: Inadequate bleaching procedure.
Remedy: Rebleach and repeat fixing, washing and drying stage

FAULTS IN PRINTING

Faults common to all types of printing are listed with those relating to black and white printing; those specific to color printing are listed under the appropriate headings. Apart from minor blemishes that can be retouched, faults in prints cannot be corrected, and the remedies described here can be applied only in subsequent printing.

Black and white printing

● **Low contrast, poor black and white tones**
Cause: Underdevelopment; paper fogged.
Remedy: Try a higher grade of paper. Check the agitation time, temperature and dilution directions of the developer. Guard against fogging the paper — don't expose it to the safelight for too long before processing, or place it too close to the safelight. Ensure that the safelight is not too strong and is of the right type, and be careful not to leave the lid of the paper box off while making a print.

● **High contrast** with compressed range of grays
Cause: Overdevelopment.
Remedy: Check the developer directions concerning agitation, time and temperature.

● **Image too dark**
Cause: Overexposure in printing; overdevelopment; paper fogged.
Remedy: Make a second test strip to confirm the exposure time. Check that the lens was stopped down to the correct aperture. Check the developer directions for the recommended time, temperature, agitation and dilution. Check that the paper stock hasn't been fogged — check the paper's box, the safelight directions and the darkroom's light-tightness.

● **White spots**
Cause: Air bubbles on the print during development.
Remedy: Agitate the print constantly while it is in the developer.

● **White branched, lightning-like marks**
Cause: Static electricity has marked the print or negative slightly.
Remedy: If the mark is on the negative, retouch the print.

● **Blue, purple or brownish stains**
Cause: Developer contaminated from fixer or stop bath.
Remedy: Remix chemicals. Avoid carry-over.

● **Dark streaks**
Cause: Excessive draining time after development; or fixer solution is too weak.
Remedy: Drain print quickly after development. Use fresh fixer solution.

● **Uneven, patchy image**
Cause: Insufficient solution level in tray; or the print was taken from the developer before fully developed, in an attempt to compensate for overexposure.
Remedy: Use more solution in each tray and check that the print is always covered by the solutions. Give all prints full development time.

● **Blotchy image with yellowish-white tones**
Cause: Old or incorrectly stored paper stock.
Remedy: Store paper on its side in a cool, dry, dark place and use it as soon as possible.

● **Light rings on the image**
Cause: Interference rings ('Newton's rings') caused by a poor fit between negative and carrier glass.
Remedy: Use a specially designed glass or use a glassless negative carrier.

Printing from color negatives

● **Overall color cast**
Cause: Wrong filtration.
Remedy: Add a combination of

filters of the same color as the cast, or remove a combination with the complementary color.

● Cyan stains
Cause: Partial contamination of developer.
Remedy: Remix developer. Avoid carry-over.

● Reddish, magenta or pink stain overall
Cause: Oxidized developer; improper storage; old solutions; insufficient wash time.
Remedy: Use fresh developer. Store solutions correctly and check the mixing date.

● Cyan or blue streaks
Cause: Developer contaminating bleach/fix.
Remedy: Thoroughly drain the print tube after the developer stage. Use clean beakers.

● Light patchy areas
Cause: Paper curled the wrong way when loaded into the print tube.
Remedy: Load paper with its emulsion inwards.

Printing from slides

Cibachrome A process

● Color cast
Cause: Incorrect filtration.
Remedy: Subtract a filter combination of the same color, or add the complementary color.

● Light image with greenish highlights, dull black shadow areas
Cause: Development time too long.
Remedy: Check processing time with directions. Check the test print.

● Foggy, dull print
Cause: Insufficient bleach time; or bleach too weak or exhausted.
Remedy: Check bleach time and dilution. Use fresh bleach if necessary.

● Dull and dark print
Cause: Contaminated bleach/fix solution.
Remedy: Remix and avoid carry-over.

● Low contrast cast
Cause: Fixer omitted, exhausted or too weak.
Remedy: Check the dilution of the fixer. Check that the fixing step was not omitted.

● Black print with no image
Cause: Bleach bath omitted.
Remedy: Use beakers and bottles in the same order to avoid missing out a step.

● Light image with overall blue cast
Cause: Developer solution too concentrated.
Remedy: Check the dilution against the manufacturer's instructions.

Ektachrome 14RC process

● Cyan cast overall
Cause: First developer contaminated with bleach/fixer.
Remedy: Remix fresh developer; avoid carry-over. Use clean chemical beakers.

● Blue or reddish cast overall
Cause: Insufficient first or second wash respectively.
Remedy: Increase the appropriate wash time, temperature and/or flow of water.

● Magenta cast on a dark print
Cause: Insufficient first development.
Remedy: Check directions for correct time, temperature, dilution and agitation.

● Blue cast in shadow areas
Cause: Insufficient color development.
Remedy: Check directions for correct time, temperature, dilution and agitation.

● Foggy, low-contrast highlights
Cause: Insufficient bleach/fix procedure; contaminated first developer.
Remedy: Check directions. Mix fresh developing solution.

GLOSSARY

Aberration. Inherent faults in a lens image. Aberrations include ASTIGMATISM, BARREL DISTORTION, CHROMATIC ABERRATION, COMA, SPHERICAL ABERRATION. COMPOUND LENSES minimize aberrations.

Accelerator. Alkali in a developer, used to speed up its action.

Actinic. (Describing light) able to affect photographic material. With ordinary film, visible light and some ultraviolet light is actinic, while infrared is not.

Acutance. Objective measure of image sharpness, depending on the suddenness of tone changes at edges in the picture.

Additive color printing. One of the two methods of filtering the enlarger light for correct color when color printing. Three successive exposures of the negative are made, with red, green and blue light respectively. See also SUBTRACTIVE COLOR PRINTING.

Air bells. Bubbles of air clinging to the emulsion surface during processing, which prevent uniform chemical action. Removed by agitation.

Airbrush. An instrument used by photographers for retouching prints. It uses a controlled flow of compressed air to spray paint or dye.

Anamorphic lens. Special type of lens which compresses the image in one dimension by means of cylindrical or prismatic elements. The image can be restored to normal by using a similar lens for printing or projection.

Angle of view. Strictly the angle subtended by the diagonal of the film at the rear NODAL POINT of the lens. Generally taken to mean the wider angle 'seen' by a given lens. The longer the focal length of a lens, the narrower its angle of view. See also COVERING POWER.

Aperture. Strictly, the opening that limits the amount of light reaching the film and hence the brightness of the image. In some cameras the aperture is fixed size; in others it is in the form opening in a barrier called the 'RAGM and can be varied in size.

(An iris diaphragm forms a continuously variable opening, while a stop plate has a number of holes of varying sizes.) Photographers, however, generally use the term 'aperture' to refer to the diameter of this opening. See also F NUMBER.

ASA. American Standards Association, which devised one of the two most commonly used systems for rating the speed of an emulsion (i.e., its sensitivity). A film rated at 400 ASA would be twice as fast as one rated at 200 ASA and four times as fast as one rated at 100 ASA. See also DIN, ISO.

Astigmatism. The inability of a lens to focus vertical and horizontal lines in the same focal plane. Corrected lenses are called 'anastigmatic'.

Automatic camera. Camera in which the exposure is automatically selected. A semi-automatic camera requires the user to pre-select the shutter speed or the aperture.

Back projection. Projection of slides on to a translucent screen from behind, instead of onto the front of, a reflective screen.

Ball-and-socket head. A type of tripod fitting that allows the camera to be secured at the required angle by fastening a single locking-screw. See also PAN-AND-TILT HEAD.

Barn doors. Hinged flaps for studio lamps, used to control the beam of light.

Barrel distortion. Lens defect characterized by the distortion of straight lines at the edges of an image so that they curve inwards at the corners of the frame.

Bas relief. In photography the name given to the special effect created when a negative and positive are sandwiched together and printed slightly out of register. The resulting picture gives the impression of being carved in low relief, like a bas-relief sculpture.

Beaded screen. Type of front-projection screen. The surface of the screen is covered with minute glass beads, giving a brighter picture than a plain white screen.

Bellows. Light-tight folding bag made of pleated cloth used on some cameras to join the lens to the camera body.

Between-the-lens shutter. One of the two main types of shutter. Situated close to the diaphragm, it consists of thin metal blades or leaves which spring open and then close when the camera is fired, exposing the film. See also FOCAL PLANE SHUTTER.

Bleaching. Chemical process for removing black metallic silver from the emulsion by converting it to a compound that may be dissolved.

Bleach out process. Technique of producing a line drawing based on a photographic image. The outlines of a photograph are drawn over with pencil or waterproof ink, then the silver image is bleached away, leaving the outline behind.

Bloom. Thin coating of metallic fluoride on the air-glass surface of a lens. It reduces reflections at that surface.

Bounced flash. Soft light achieved by aiming flash at a wall or ceiling to avoid the harsh shadows that result if the light is pointed directly at the subject.

Bracketing. Technique of ensuring perfect exposure by taking several photographs of the same subject at slightly different settings.

Bromide paper. Photographic paper for printing enlargements. The basic light-sensitive ingredient in the emulsion is silver bromide.

B setting. Setting of the shutter speed dial of a camera at which the shutter remains open for as long as the release button is held down, allowing longer exposures than the preset speeds on the camera. The 'B' stands for 'brief' or 'bulb' (for historical reasons). See also T SETTING.

BSI. British Standards Institution, which has an independent system of rating emulsion speed, similar to the ASA system. However, the BSI system is used industrially.

Bulk loader. Device for handling film which has been bought in bulk as a single length and which needs to be cut and loaded into cassettes.

Burning in. Technique used in printing photographs when a small area of the print requires more exposure than the rest. After normal exposure the main area is shielded with a card or by the hands while the detail (e.g., a highlight which is too dense on the negative) receives further exposure. DODGING is the reverse technique.

Cable release. Simple camera accessory used to reduce camera vibrations when the shutter is released, particularly when the camera is supported by a tripod and a relatively long exposure is being used. It consists of a short length of thin cable attached at one end to the release button of the camera; the cable is encased in a flexible rubber or metal tube and is operated by a plunger.

Callier effect. Phenomenon which accounts for the higher contrast produced by enlargers using a condenser system as compared with those using a diffuser system. This effect, first investigated by André Callier in 1909, is explained by the fact that the light, focused by the condenser onto the lens of the enlarger, is partly scattered by the negative before it reaches the lens; and because the denser parts of the negative scatter the most light, the contrast is increased. In a diffuser enlarger, on the other hand, all areas of the negative cause the same amount of scattering.

Calotype. Print made by an early photographic process using paper negatives. Iodized paper requiring lengthy exposure was used in the camera. The system was patented by Fox Talbot in 1841, but became obsolete with the introduction of the COLLODION PROCESS. Also known as Talbotype.

Camera movements. Adjustme
the relative positions of the len
film whereby the geometry c
image can be controlled. A
movements is a particula
view cameras, though a

cameras allow limited movements, and special lenses are available which do the same for 35mm cameras.

Camera obscura. Literally a 'dark chamber'. An optical system, familiar before the advent of photographic materials, using a pinhole or a lens to project an image onto a screen. One form of camera obscura, designed as an artists' aid, is the ancestor of the modern camera.

Canada balsam. Resin used to cement together pieces of optical glass, such as elements of a lens. When set it has a refractive index almost exactly equal to that of glass. It is obtained from the balsam fir of North America.

Cartridge. Plastic container of film, either 126 or 110. The film is wound from one spool to a second spool inside the cartridge.

Cassette. Container for 35mm film. After exposure the film is wound back onto the spool of the cassette before the camera is opened.

Cast. Overall shift towards a particular hue, giving color photographs an unnatural appearance.

CdS cell. Photosensitive cell used in one type of light meter, incorporating a cadmium sulphide resistor, which regulates an electric current. See also SELENIUM CELL.

Center-weighted meter. Type of through-the-lens light meter. The reading is most strongly influenced by the intensity of light at the center of the image.

Chlorobromide papers. Printing papers coated with a compound of silver bromide and silver chloride, giving warm tones.

Chromatic aberration. The inability of ̄ens to focus different colors on the ̄e focal plane.

̄genic. Chromogenic means ̄color forming', and ̄ic films and papers are ̄hich the final image is ̄d dyes formed during ̄r than silver.

Chromopathic. See DYE DESTRUCTION.

Circle of confusion. Disc of light in the image produced by a lens when a point on the subject is not perfectly brought into focus. The eye cannot distinguish between a very small circle of confusion (of diameter less than 0.01in) and a true point.

Close-up lens. Simple positive lens placed over the normal lens to magnify the image. The strength of the close-up lens is measured in diopters. Also known as SUPPLEMENTARY LENS.

Cold cathode enlarger. Type of enlarger using as its light source a special fluorescent tube with a low working temperature. Particularly suitable for large-format work.

Collodion process. Wet-plate photographic process introduced in 1851 by F. Scott Archer, remaining in use until the 1880s. It superseded DAGUERREOTYPE and CALOTYPE.

Color analyser. Electronic device which assesses the correct filtration for a color print.

Color conversion filters. Camera filters required when daylight color film is used in artificial light, or when film balanced for artificial light is used in daylight.

Color correction filters. Filters used to correct slight irregularities in specific light sources (e.g., electronic flash). The name is als used to describe the cyan, magenta and yellow filters which are used to balance the color of prints made from color negatives.

Color negative film. Film giving color negatives intended for printing.

Color reversal film. Film giving color positives (i.e., slides or transparencies) directly. Prints can also be made from the positive transparencies.

Color temperature. Measure of the relative blueness of redness of a light source, expressed in KELVINS. The color temperature is the temperature to which a theoretical 'black body' would have to be heated to give out light of the same color.

Coma. A lens defect which results in off-axis points of light appearing in the image not as points but as discs with comet-like tails.

Combination printing. General term for techniques in which more than one negative is printed onto a single sheet of paper.

Compound lens. Lens consisting of more than one element, designed so that the faults of the various elements largely cancel each other out.

Condenser. Optical system consisting of one or two plano-convex lenses (flat on one side, curved outwards on the other) used in an enlarger or side projector to concentrate light from a source and focus it onto the negative or slide. The system increases print contrast and cuts exposure times.

Contact print. Print which is the same size as the negative, made by sandwiching together the negative and the photographic paper when making the print.

Converging lens. Any lens that is thicker in the middle than at the edges. The name derives from the ability of such lenses to cause parallel light to converge on to a point of focus, giving an image. Also known as a positive lens. See also DIVERGING LENS.

Converging verticals. Distorted appearance of vertical lines in the image, produced when the camera is tilted upwards; tall objects such as buildings appear to be leaning backward. Can be partially corrected at the printing stage, or by the use of CAMERA MOVEMENTS.

Converter. Auxiliary lens, usually fitted between the camera body and the principal lens, giving a combined focal length that is greater than that of the principal lens alone. Most converters increase focal length by a factor of two or three.

Convertible lens. Compound lens consisting of two lens assemblies which are used separately or together. The two sections are usually of differing focal lengths, giving three possible permutations.

Correction filter. Colored filter used over the camera lens to modify the tonal balance of a black and white image; the same term is also used for COLOR CORRECTION FILTERS.

Covering power. The largest image area of acceptable quality that a given lens produces. The covering power of a lens is normally only slightly greater than the standard negative size for which it is intended, except in the case of a lens designed for use on a camera with movements (see CAMERA MOVEMENTS), when the covering power must be considerably greater.

Cropping. Enlarging only a selected portion of the negative instead of printing the entire area.

Daguerreotype. Early photographic picture made on a copper plate coated with polished silver and sensitized with silver iodide. The image was developed using mercury vapor, giving a direct positive. The process was introduced by Louis Daguerre in 1839, and was the first to be commercially successful.

Daylight film. Color film balanced to give accurate color rendering in average daylight, that is to say, when the COLOR TEMPERATURE of the light source is around 5500 Kelvins. Also suitable for use with electronic flash and blue flashbulbs.

Density. The light-absorbing power of a photographic image. A logarithmic scale is used in measurements: 50 per cent absorption is expressed as 0.3, 100 per cent is 1.0, etc. In general terms, density is simply the opaqueness of a negative or the blackness of a print.

Depth of field. Zone of acceptable sharpness extending in front of and behind the point on the subject which is exactly focused by the lens.

Depth of focus. Very narrow zone on the image side of the lens within which slight variations in the position of the film will make no appreciable difference to the focusing of the

Developer. Chemical agent converts the LATENT IMAGE visible image. In addition

developing agent that reduces the exposed halides to black metallic silver, the developer solution usually contains an accelerator (an alkali which helps to speed up the action); a preservative (to prolong the life of the developer); and a restrainer (which helps to control development and prevent fogging).

Developer improvers. Chemicals with anti-fog properties that can be added to developing solutions or may already be included in the ingredients of a developer.

Diaphragm. System of adjustable metal blades forming a roughly circular opening of variable diameter, used to control the APERTURE of a lens.

Diapositive. Alternative name for TRANSPARENCY.

Dichroic fog. Processing fault characterized by a stain of reddish and greenish colors — hence the name 'dichroic' (literally, 'two-colored'). Caused by the use of exhausted FIXER whose acidity is insufficient to halt the development entirely. A fine deposit of silver is formed which appears reddish by transmitted light and greenish by reflected light.

Differential focusing. Technique involving the use of shallow DEPTH OF FIELD to enhance the illusion of depth and solidity in a photograph. Useful for blurring unwanted elements.

Diffraction. Phenomenon occurring when light passes close to the edge of an opaque body or through a narrow aperture. The light is slightly deflected setting up interference patterns which may sometimes be seen by the naked eye as fuzziness. The effect is occasionally noticeable in photography, as when, for example, a very small lens aperture is used.

⬩IN. Deutsche Industrie Norm, the ⬩rman standards association, which ⬩ed one of the two widely used ⬩s for rating the speed of an ⬩n (see also ASA). On the DIN ⬩ry increase of 3 indicates that ⬩ty of the emulsion has ⬩DIN is equivalent to 100 ⬩SO.

Diverging lens. Any lens that is thicker at the edges than in the middle. Such lenses cause parallel rays of light to diverge, forming an image on the same side of the lens as the subject. Diverging lenses are also known as negative lenses.

D-max. Technical term for the maximum density of which an emulsion is capable.

Dodging. Technique, also known as shading, used in printing photographs when one area of the print requires less exposure than the rest. A hand or a sheet of card is used to prevent the selected area receiving the full exposure. See also BURNING IN.

Drift-by technique. Processing technique used to allow for the cooling of a chemical bath (normally the developer) during the time it is in contact with the emulsion. Before use, the solution is warmed to a point slightly above the required temperature, so that while it is being used it cools to a temperature slightly below, but still within the margin of safety.

Drying marks. Blemishes on the emulsion resulting from uneven drying; also, residue on the film after water from the wash has evaporated.

Dry mounting. Method of mounting prints onto card backing, using a special heat-sensitive adhesive tissue.

Dye coupler. Chemical responsible for producing the appropriate colored dyes during the development of a color photograph. Dye couplers may be incorporated in the emulsion; or they may be part of the developer.

Dye destruction process. System for forming color images by selectively eliminating dyes during processing. It makes use of a tripack material in which the three dyes are ready-formed before exposure. After exposure, a bleaching agent is used to destroy the dyes in proportion to the development of the silver halide image. Dyes are therefore destroyed most in exposed areas. This means it is possible to produce positive prints from color transparencies without reversal.

Edge effects. Development phenomena characterized by increased contrast at the boundaries of areas with markedly different densities. The effects are produced when developer becomes rapidly exhausted in heavily exposed areas, and fresher developer from the adjacent area moves across to replace it. Thus the edge of the heavily exposed area receives more development than the average for that area (the displaced fresh developer penetrating only slightly into the area), and the edge of the adjacent, lightly exposed area receives less development than the average for that area, some of its development potential having been lost to the edge of the heavily exposed area. The resulting increased sharpness is an effect called ACUTANCE that is sometimes sought after, and can be emphasized by using a developer that exhausts rapidly and by avoiding agitation.

Electronic flash. Type of flashgun which uses the flash of light produced by a high-voltage electrical discharge between two electrodes in a gas-filled tube. See also FLASHBULB.

Emulsion. In photography, the light-sensitive layer of a photographic material. The emulsion consists essentially of SILVER HALIDE crystals suspended in GELATIN.

Enlargement. Photographic print larger than the original image on the film. See also CONTACT PRINT.

Exposure. Total amount of light allowed to reach the light-sensitive material during the formation of the LATENT IMAGE. The exposure is dependent on the brightness of the image, the camera APERTURE and on the length of time for which the material is exposed.

Exposure meter. Instrument for measuring the intensity of light so as to determine the correct SHUTTER and APERTURE settings.

Extension tubes. Accessories used in close-up photography, consisting of metal tubes that can be fitted between the lens and the camera body, thus increasing the lens-to-film distance.

Farmer's reducer. See REDUCTION.

Fast lens. Lens of wide maximum aperture, relative to its focal length. The current state of lens design and manufacture determines the standards by which a lens is considered 'fast' for its focal length.

Fill-in. Additional lighting used to supplement the principal light source and brighten shadows.

Film speed. A film's degree of sensitivity to light. Usually expressed as a rating on either the ASA or the DIN scales.

Filter. Transparent sheet, usually of glass or gelatin, used to block a specific part of the light passing through it, or to change or distort the image in some way. See also COLOR CONVERSION FILTERS, COLOR CORRECTION FILTERS, CORRECTION FILTERS and POLARIZING FILTERS.

Filter pack. Assembly of filters used in an enlarger when making color prints. Normally consists of any two of the three subtractive primaries (yellow, magenta, cyan) in the appropriate strengths.

Fisheye lens. Extreme wide-angle lens, with an ANGLE OF VIEW of about 180°. Since its DEPTH OF FIELD is almost infinite, there is no need for any focusing, but it produces images that are highly distorted.

Fixed-focus lens. Lens permanently focused at a fixed point, usually at the hyperfocal distance. Most cheap cameras use this system, giving sharp pictures from about 7ft (2 metres) to infinity.

Fixer. Chemical bath needed to fix the photographic image permanently after it has been developed. The fixer stabilizes the emulsion by converting the undeveloped SILVER HALIDES into water-soluble compounds, which can then be dissolved out.

Flare. Light reflected inside the camera or between the elements lens, giving rise to irregular ma the negative and degrading t of the image. It is to some ex overcome by using bloomed lenses (see BLOOM).

Flashbulb. Expendable bulb with a filament of metal foil which is designed to burn up very rapidly giving a brief, intense flare of light, sufficiently bright to allow a photograph to be taken. Most flashbulbs have a light blue plastic coating, which gives the flash a COLOR TEMPERATURE close to that of daylight.

Flashing. Technique involving deliberately fogging a print briefly with white light during exposure. The effect is to control contrast. The extra exposure may be spread equally over the whole print, producing a soft overall effect; it may be used for vignetting so that the image merges into a black border; or it may be directed to a particular area by means of a torch to cause local darkening.

Floodlight. General term for artificial light source which provides a constant and continuous output of light, suitable for studio photography or similar work. Usually consists of a 125-500W tungsten-filament lamp mounted in a reflector.

F-number. Number resulting when the focal length of a lens is divided by the diameter of the aperture. A sequence of f-numbers, marked on the ring or dial which controls the diaphragm, is used to calibrate the aperture in regular steps (known as STOPS) between its smallest and largest settings. The f-numbers generally follow a standard sequence such that the interval between one stop and the next represents a halving or doubling in the image brightness. As f-numbers represent fractions, the numbers become progressively higher as the aperture is reduced to allow in less light.

Focal length. Distance between the optical center of a lens and the point at which rays of light parallel to the optical axis are brought to a focus. In general, greater the focal length of a lens, smaller its ANGLE OF VIEW.

...ane. Plane on which a given ... brought to a sharp focus; in ... rms, the plane where the ... ned.

Focal-plane shutter. One of the two main types of shutter, used almost universally in SINGLE-LENS REFLEX CAMERAS. Positioned behind the lens (though in fact slightly in front of the focal plane) the shutter consists of a system of cloth blinds or metal blades; when the camera is fired, a slit travels across the image area either vertically or horizontally. The width and speed of travel of the slit determine the duration of the exposure.

Fog. Veiling of an image caused by accidentally exposing the film or paper; by overactive developer or weak fixer containing heavy deposits of silver salts; by overlong storage; or by exposure to powerful X-rays.

Forced development. Technique used to increase the effective speed of a film by extending its normal development time. Also known as 'pushing' the film.

Format. Dimensions of the image recorded on film by a given type of camera. The term may also refer to the dimensions of a print.

Fresnel lens. Lens whose surface consists of a series of concentric circular 'steps', each of which is shaped like part of the surface of a convex lens. Fresnel lenses are often used in the viewing screens of single-lens reflex cameras and for spotlights.

Gelatin. Colloid material used as binding medium for the emulsion of photographic paper and film; also used in some types of filter.

Glazing. Process by which glossy prints can be given a shiny finish by being dried in contact with a hot drum or plate of chromium or steel.

Grain. Granular texture appearing to some degree in all processed photographic materials. In black and white photographs the grains are minute particles of black metallic silver which constitute the dark areas of a photograph. In color photographs the silver has been removed chemically, but tiny blotches of dye retain the appearance of graininess. The faster the film, the coarser the grain. It can produce arresting pictorial effects.

Granularity. Objective measure of graininess.

Guide number. Number indicating the effective power of a flash unit. For a given film speed, the guide number divided by the distance between the flash and the subject gives the appropriate F NUMBER to use.

Halation. Phenomenon characterized by halo-like band around the developed image of a bright light source. Caused by internal reflection of light from the support of the emulsion (i.e., the paper of the print or the base layer of a film).

Half-frame. Film format measuring 24x18mm, half the size of standard format 35mm pictures.

Halogens. A particular group of chemical elements, among which chlorine, bromine and iodine are included. These elements are important in photography because their compounds with silver (SILVER HALIDES) form the light-sensitive substances in all photographic materials.

Hardener. Chemical used to strengthen the gelatin of an emulsion against physical damage.

High-contrast developers. Highly alkaline developers using hydroquinone alone as developing agent. They yield very high contrast results, especially with lith films.

High-key. Containing predominantly light tones. See also LOW-KEY.

High-speed processing. Method of rapid developing and fixing of photographic materials when conventional processing techniques are too slow, for example for newspapers. Some people make up their own solution of such developers as Ilford's liquid Autophen, ID11 or Microphen, warmed to just below the point where chemical fog might be a hazard. Negatives can be developed in 20 seconds, fixed in two minutes with a rapid fixer, and dried in two minutes. Monobath developers, which also incorporate a fixing agent, can develop and fix a black and white film in three minutes while still in the cassette and in daylight; a disadvantage is a considerable loss of contrast.

Highlights. Brightest area of the subject, or corresponding areas of an image; in the negative these are areas of greatest density.

Holography. Technique whereby information is recorded on a photographic plate as an interference pattern which, when viewed under the appropriate conditions, yields a three-dimensional image. Holography bears little relation to conventional photography except in its use of a light-sensitive film.

Hot-shoe. Accessory shoe on a camera which incorporates a live contact for firing a flashgun, thus eliminating the need for a separate contact.

Hue. The quality that distinguishes between colors of the same saturation and brightness; the quality, for example, of redness or greenness.

Hypo. Popular name for sodium thiosulphate, once the universal fixing agent for dissolving unwanted silver halides. A hypo eliminator (HE) is an oxidizing agent that converts the hypo into harmless sodium sulphate, thus ensuring the hypo is thoroughly eliminated.

Incident light. Light falling on the subject. When a subject is being photographed, readings may be taken of the incident light instead of the reflected light.

Infrared radiation. Part of the spectrum of electromagnetic radiation, having wavelengths longer than visible red light (approximately 700 to 15,000 nanometres). Infrared radiation is felt as heat, and can be recorded on special types of photographic film. See IR SETTING.

Integral tripack. Composite photographic emulsion used in virtually all color films and papers, comprising three layers, each of which is sensitive to one of the three primary colors.

Intermittency effect. Phenome-

observed when an emulsion is given a series of brief exposures. The density of the image thus produced is lower than the image density produced by a single exposure of duration equal to the total of the short exposures.

Inverse square law. Law stating that, for a point source of light, the intensity of light decreases with the square of the distance from the source, thus, when the distance is doubled, the intensity is reduced by a factor of four.

Indicator. Chemicals added to a processing bath to indicate certain features about its effectiveness and condition (particularly the pH factor).

Intensification. Technique of increasing the image density of a thin black and white negative, either with a chemical or dye intensifier, or by optical means. In the chemical process the negative is immersed in chemical baths that increase the size of the silver halide grains. This increases contrast. Silver areas of the image can also be treated with dye toners, increasing the opacity of the negative and thus partially stopping the lightwaves passing from the enlarger to the print. Optical treatment by IRRADIATION consists of photographing the negative by a raking side light.

IR (infrared) setting. A mark sometimes found on the focusing ring of a camera, indicating a shift in focus needed for infrared photography. INFRARED RADIATION is refracted less than visible light, and the infrared image is therefore brought to a focus slightly behind the visible image.

Irradiation. Internal scattering of light inside photographic emulsions during exposure, caused by reflections from the SILVER HALIDE crystals.

ISO (International Standards Organisation). System of rating emulsion speeds which is superseding ASA and DIN. 100ASA/DIN21 equals 100ISO.

.ule. Unit of energy in the SI (Système ...ernational) system of units. The joule ...ed in photography to indicate the ...t of an electronic flash.

Kelvin (K). Unit of temperature in the SI system of units. The Kelvin scale begins at absolute zero (-273°C) and uses degrees equal in magnitude to 1°C. Kelvins are used in photography to express color temperature.

Laser. Acronym for Light Amplification by Stimulated Emission of Radiation. Devide for producing an intense beam of coherent light that is of a single very pure color. Used in the production of holograms (see HOLOGRAPHY).

Latensification. Technique used to increase effective film speed by fogging the film, either chemically or with light, between exposure and development.

Latent image. Invisible image recorded on photographic emulsion as a result of exposure to light. The latent image is converted into a visible image by the action of a DEVELOPER.

Latitude. Tolerance of photographic material to variations in exposure.

Lens hood. Simple lens accessory, usually made of rubber or light metal, used to shield the lens from light coming from areas outside the field of view. Such light is the source of FLARE.

Lith film. Ultrahigh-contrast film used to eliminate gray tones and reduce the image to areas of pure black or pure white.

Long-focus lens. Lens of focal length greater than that of the STANDARD LENS for a given format. Long-focus lenses have a narrow field of view, and consequently make distant objects appear closer. See also TELEPHOTO LENS.

Low-key. Containing predominantly dark tones. See also HIGH KEY.

Mackie line. Line appearing around a highlight on a silver halide emulsion. It is produced by the lateral diffusion of exhausted developer that causes EDGE EFFECTS. See also SABATTIER EFFECT.

Macro lens. Strictly, a lens capable of giving a 1:1 magnification ratio (a life-size image); the term is generally used to describe any close-focusing lens. Macro lenses can also be used at ordinary subject distances.

Macrophotography. Close up photography in the range of magnification between life-size and about ten times life-size.

Magnification ratio. Ratio of image size to object size. The magnification ratio is sometimes useful in determining the correct exposure in close-up and macrophotography.

Masking. Term used to describe ways in which light is prevented from reaching selected areas of an image for various purposes. Some enlargers, for example, incorporate masking devices that cut down stray light passing around the negative or transparency. A masking frame is placed beneath the enlarger lens to establish print size, determine proportions of the picture and keep the paper flat.

Mercury vapor lamp. Type of light source sometimes used in studio photography, giving a bluish light. The light is produced by passing an electric current through a tube filled with mercury vapor.

Metol. Developing agent, available under various brand names. It is a white crystalline powder, that may cause an allergic reaction.

Microphotography. Technique used to copy documents and similar materials on to a very small-format film, so that a large amount of information may be stored compactly. The term is sometimes also used to refer to the technique of taking photographs through a microscope, otherwise known as PHOTOMICROGRAPHY.

Microprism. Special type of focusing screen composed of a grid of tiny prisms, often incorporated into the viewing screens of SLR cameras. The microprism gives a fragmented image when the image is out of focus.

Mired. Acronym for Micro-Reciprocal Degree. Unit on a scale of COLOR TEMPERATURE used to calibrate COLOR CORRECTION FILTERS. The mired value

of a light is given by the express: one million ÷ color temperature in Kelvins.

Mirror lens. Long-focus lens of extremely compact design whose construction is based on a combination of lenses and curved mirrors. Light rays from the subject are reflected backwards and forwards inside the barrel of the lens before reaching the film. Also known as a catadioptric lens.

Monobath. See HIGH-SPEED PROCESSING.

Montage. Composite photographic image made from several different pictures by physically assembling them or printing them successively onto a single piece of paper.

Motor drive. Battery powered camera accessory, used to wind on the film automatically after each shot, capable of achieving several frames per second.

MQ/PQ developers. Popular general purpose developing solutions containing metol and hydroquinone or phenidone and hydroquinone.

Multigrade paper. See VARIABLE CONTRACT PAPER.

Negative. Image in which light tones are recorded as dark, and vice versa; in color negatives every color in the original subject is represented by its complementary color.

Negative lens. See DIVERGING LENS.

Neutral density filter. Uniformly gray filter which reduces the brightness of an image without altering its color content. Used in conjunction with lenses that have no diaphragm to control the aperture (such as MIRROR LENSES), or when the light is too bright for the speed of film used.

Newton's rings. Narrow multicolored bands that appear when two transparent surfaces are sandwiched together with imperfect contact. The pattern is caused by interference and can be troublesome when slides or negatives are held between glass or plastic.

Nodal point. Point of intersection between the optical axis of a compound lens and one of the two principal planes of refraction: a compound lens thus has a front and a rear nodal point, from which its basic measurements (such as focal length) are made.

Normal lens. See STANDARD LENS.

Opacity. Objective measurement of the degree of opaqueness of a material; the ratio of incident light to transmitted light.

Open flash. Technique of firing flash manually after the camera shutter has been opened instead of synchronizing the two.

Optical axis. Imaginary line through the optical center of a lens system.

Orthochromatic. Term used to describe black and white emulsions that are insensitive to red light. See also PANCHROMATIC.

Oxidation. Chemical reaction in which a substance combines with oxygen. Developer tends to deteriorate as a result of oxidation unless stored in airtight containers.

Pan-and-tilt head. Type of tripod head employing independent locking mechanisms for movement in two planes at right angles to each other. Thus the camera can be locked in one plane while remaining free to move in the other.

Panchromatic. Term used to describe black and white photographic emulsions that are sensitive to all the visible colors (although not uniformly so). Most modern films are panchromatic. See also ORTHOCHROMATIC.

Panning. Technique of swinging the camera to follow a moving subject, ...d to convey the impression of ...d. A relatively slow shutter speed ...d, so that a sharp image of the ... object is recorded against a ...background.

...camera. Special design of camera whose lens moves slowly through an arc during exposure, covering a long stretch of film.

Parallax. Apparent displacement of an object brought about by a change in viewpoint. Parallax error is apparent in close-ups only, shown in the discrepancy between the image produced by the lens and the view seen through the viewfinder in cameras where the viewfinder and taking lens are separate.

Pentaprism. Five-sided prism used in the construction of eye-level viewfinders for SLR cameras, providing a laterally correct, upright image. (In practice many pentaprisms have more than five sides, since unnecessary parts of the prism are cut off to reduce its bulk.)

Permanence. Permanence is determined initially by the effectiveness of the processing, and in color photographs by the stability of the dyes in the emulsion layers. Development and fixing must be followed by thorough washing to remove all traces of those residual silver compounds that could affect the image's appearance. If prints are to be mounted, dry mounting is the most permanent method because it does not introduce any potentially harmful chemicals to the back of the print, as do many glues. When processed and stored carefully, black and white photographic materials will generally stay in good condition indefinitely. Color images are less permanent, and are especially susceptible to direct sunlight. For maximum life expectancy, color images should be stored in refrigerated conditions or as separation negatives.

Phenidone. Developing agent, usually used to stimulate the action of hydroquinone, in place of metol. A small amount is very effective.

pH value. Strictly, the logarithm of the concentration of hydrogen ions in grams per litre. Used as a scale of acidity or alkalinity of a substance. Water is neutral at pH 7.

Photo-electric cell. Light-sensitive cell used in the circuit of a light meter. Some types of photo-electric cell generate an electric current when stimulated by light; others react by a change in their electrical resistance.

Photoflood. Bright tungsten filament bulb used as an artificial light source in photography. The bulb is over-run and so has a short life.

Photogram. Photographic image produced by arranging objects on the surface of a sheet of photographic paper or film, or so that they cast a shadow directly onto the material as it is being exposed. The image is thus produced without the use of a lens.

Photometer. Instrument for measuring the intensity of light by comparing it with a standard source.

Photomicrography. Technique of taking photographs through the lens of a microscope, used to achieve magnifications greater than those obtainable using a MACRO LENS.

Physiogram. Photographic image of the pattern traced out by a light source suspended from a pendulum. The pattern depends on the arrangement and complexity of the pendulum.

Pinhole camera. Simple camera which employs a very small hole instead of a lens to form an image. Pinhole cameras are principally used as a simple demonstration of the idea that light travels in straight lines; but they can take photographs.

Polarizing filter. Thin transparent filter used as a lens accessory to cut down reflections from certain shiny surfaces (notably glass and water) or to intensify the color of a blue sky. Polarizing filters are made of a material that will polarize light passing through it and which will also block a proportion of light that has already been polarized; rotating the filter will vary the proportion that is blocked.

Polarized light. Light whose electrical vibrations are confined to a single plane. In everyday conditions, light is usually unpolarized, having electrical (and magnetic) vibrations in every plane. Light reflected from shiny non-metallic surfaces which makes it difficult to distinguish color and detail is frequently polarized and can be controlled with a POLARIZING FILTER.

Positive. Image in which the light tones correspond to the light areas of the subject, and the dark tones correspond to the dark areas; in a positive color image, the colors of the subject are also represented by the same colors in the image. See NEGATIVE.

Positive lens. See CONVERGING LENS.

Posterization. Technique of drastically simplifying the tones of an image by making several negatives from an original, with different densities, contrasts, etc., and then sandwiching them together and printing them in register.

Primary colors. In the ADDITIVE SYNTHESIS of color, blue, green and red. Lights of these colors can be mixed together to give white light or light of any other color.

Process film. Slow, fine-grained film of good resolving power, used for copying work.

Process lens. Highly corrected lens designed specially for copying work.

Pushing. Technique of extending the development of a film so as to increase its effective speed or to improve contrast.

Rangefinder. Optical device for measuring distance, often coupled to the focusing mechanism of a camera lens. A rangefinder displays two images, showing the scene from slightly different viewpoints, which must be superimposed to establish the measurement of distance.

Real image. In optics, the term used to describe an image that can be formed on a screen, as distinct from a VIRTUAL IMAGE. The rays of light actually pass through the image before entering the eye of the observer.

Reciprocity law. Principle according to which the density of the image formed when an emulsion is develop is directly proportional to the durat of the exposure and the intensity of the light. However, with extremely short or long exposures and with unusual light intensities the reciprocity law fails to apply and unpredictable results occur. See also INTERMITTENCY EFFECT.

Reducer. Chemical agent used to reduce the density of a developed image either uniformly over the whole surface (leaving the contrast unaltered) or in proportion to the existing density (thus decreasing contrast).

Reduction. Technique for thinning an overdense negative or print with the aid of a chemical solution such as Farmer's reducer, which bleaches away the silver image. Reducer can brighten small areas of a print, or rescue a muddy or overexposed print immersed in the solution. But reducer affects lighter tones first, thereby increasing contrast. After reduction the print must be fixed again and washed.

Reflector. In photography, the sheets of white, gray or silverized card employed to reflect light into shadow areas, usually in studio lighting arrangements.

Reflex camera. Generic name for types of camera whose viewing systems employ a mirror to reflect an image onto a screen. See TWIN-LENS REFLEX CAMERA and SINGLE-LENS REFLEX CAMERA.

Refraction. Bending of a ray of light travelling obliquely from one medium to another; the ray is refracted at the surface of the two media. The angle through which a ray will be bent can be calculated from the refractive indices of the media.

Rehalogenization. The process of converting deposits of black metallic silver back into silver halides. This process may be used to bleach prints in preparation for toning. (See TONER).

Resin-coated (RC) paper.
Photographic printing paper coated with synthetic resin to prevent the paper base absorbing liquids during processing. Resin-coated papers can be washed and dried more quickly than untreated papers, but are more difficult to retouch.

Resolving power. Ability of an optical system to distinguish between objects that are very close together; also used in photography to describe this ability in a film or paper emulsion.

Reticulation. Fine, irregular pattern appearing on the surface of an emulsion which has been subjected to a sudden and severe change in temperature or in the relative acidity/alkalinity of the processing solutions.

Retina. Light-sensitive layer at the back of the eye.

Reversal film. Photographic film which, when processed, gives a positive image; that is, intended for producing slides rather than negatives.

Reversing ring. Camera accessory which enables the lens to be attached back to front. Used in close-up photography to achieve higher image quality and greater magnification.

Ring flash. Type of electronic flash unit which fits around the lens to produce flat, shadowless lighting; particularly useful in close-up work. It produces an image soft and lacking in contrast.

Rising front. One of the principal CAMERA MOVEMENTS. The lens is moved vertically in a plane parallel to the film. Particularly important in architectural photography, where a rising front enables the photographer to include the top of a tall building without distorting the vertical lines. See also CONVERGING VERTICALS.

Sabattier effect. Partial reversal of the tones of a photographic image resulting from a secondary exposure to light during development. Sometimes also known as SOLARIZATION or, more correctly, pseudo-solarization, it can be used to give special printing effects.

Safelight. Special darkroom lamp whose light is of a color (such as red or orange) that will not affect certain photographic materials. Not all materials can be handled under a safelight, and some require a particular type of safelight designed specifically for them.

Sandwiching. The projection or printing of two or more negatives or slides together to produce a composite image.

Saturated color. Pure color free from any admixture of gray.

Selenium cell. One of the principal types of photoelectric cell used in light meters. A selenium cell produces a current when stimulated by light proportional to the intensity of the light.

Separation negative. A negative that records one of the three primary colors of a subject, or, more usually, a transparency, as a silver image. For photomechanical printing a set of three separation negatives is produced, recording the red, green and blue components respectively, together with a negative recording the tones of the whole scene. These are used to produce four plates in cyan, magenta, yellow and black-and-white.

Shading. Alternative term for DODGING.

Shutter. Camera mechanism which controls the duration of the exposure. The two principal types of shutter are BETWEEN-THE-LENS SHUTTERS and FOCAL-PLANE SHUTTERS.

Silver halide. Chemical compound of silver with a HALOGEN (for example, silver iodide, silver bromide or silver chloride). Silver bromide is the principal light-sensitive constituent of modern photographic emulsion, though other silver halides are also used.

Single-lens reflex (SLR) camera. One of the most popular types of camera design. Its name derives from its viewfinder system, which enables the user to see the image produced by the same lens that is used for taking the photograph. A hinged mirror reflects this image onto a viewing screen, where the picture may be composed and focused; when the shutter is released, the mirror flips out of the light path while the film is being exposed.

Slave unit. Photoelectric device used to trigger electronic flash units in studio work. The slave unit detects light from a primary flashgun linked directly to the

camera, and fires the secondary flash unit to which it is connected.

SLR. Abbreviation of SINGLE-LENS REFLEX CAMERA.

Snoot. Conical lamp attachment used to control the beam of a studio light.

Soft focus. Slight diffusion of the image achieved by the use of a special filter or similar means, giving softening of the definition. Soft-focus effects are generally used to give a gentle, romantic haze to a photograph.

Solarization. Strictly, the complete or partial reversal of the tones of an image as a result of extreme overexposure. See also SABATTIER EFFECT.

Spectrum. The multicolored band obtained when light is split up into its component WAVELENGTHS, as when a prism is used to split white light into colored rays; the term may also refer to the complete range of electromagnetic radiation, extending from the shortest to the longest wavelengths and including visible light.

Speed. The sensitivity of an emulsion as measured on one of the various scales (see ASA and DIN); or the maximum aperture of which a given lens is capable.

Spherical aberration. Lens defect resulting in an unsharp image, caused by light rays passing through the outer edges of a lens being more strongly refracted than those passing through the central parts; not all rays, therefore, are brought to exactly the same focus.

Spot meter. Special type of light meter which takes a reading from a very narrow angle of view; in some TTL METERS the reading may be taken from only a small central portion of the image in the viewfinder.

Spotting. Retouching a print or negative to remove spots and blemishes.

Stabilization. Chemical process of making the unexposed silver halides stable in prints. Used instead of fixing and washing when speed is more important than permanence.

Standard lens. Lens of focal length approximately equal to the diagonal of the negative format for which it is intended. In the case of 35mm cameras the standard lens usually has a focal length in the range of 50-55mm, slightly greater than the actual diagonal of a full frame negative (about 43mm).

Stop. Alternative name for aperture setting or F-NUMBER.

Stop bath. Weak acidic solution used in processing as an intermediate bath between the DEVELOPER and the FIXER. The stop bath serves to halt the development completely, and at the same time to neutralize the alkaline developer, thereby preventing it lowering the acidity of the fixer when it is added.

Stopping down. Colloquial term for reducing the aperture of the lens. See also STOP.

Subminiature camera. Camera using 16mm film to take negatives measuring 12×17mm.

Subtractive color printing. Principal method of filtration used in making prints from color negatives. The color balance of the print is established by exposing the paper through a suitable combination of yellow, magenta or cyan filters, which selectively block the part of the light giving rise to an unwanted color CAST.

Supplementary lens. Simple POSITIVE LENS used as an accessory for close-ups. The supplementary lens fits over the normal lens, producing a slightly magnified image.

Telephoto lens. Strictly, a special type of LONG-FOCUS LENS, having an optical construction which consists of two lens groups, the front group acts as a converging sytem, while the rear group diverges the light rays. This construction results in the lens being physically shorter than its effective focal length.

st strip. Print showing the effects of ral trial exposure times, made in to establish the correct exposure final print.

TLR. Abbreviation of TWIN-LENS REFLEX CAMERA.

Tone separation. Technique similar to POSTERIZATION, used to strengthen the tonal range registered in a print by printing the highlights and the shadows separately.

Toner. Chemical used to alter the color of a black and white print. There are four principal types of toner, each requiring a different process for treating the print. Almost any color can be achieved through the use of the appropriate toner.

Transparency. A photograph viewed by transmitted, rather than reflected, light. When mounted in a rigid frame, the transparency is called a slide.

T setting. Abbreviation of 'time' setting — a mark on some shutter controls. The T setting is used for long exposures when the photographer wishes to leave the camera with its shutter open. The first time the shutter release is pressed, the shutter opens; it remains open until the release is pressed a second time. See also B SETTING.

TTL meter. Through-the-lens meter. Built-in exposure meter which measures the intensity of light in the image produced by the main camera lens. Principally found in more sophisticated designs of SINGLE-LENS REFLEX CAMERAS.

Twin-lens reflex (TLR) camera. Type of camera whose viewing system employs a secondary lens of focal length equal to that of the main 'taking' lens: a fixed mirror reflects the image from the viewing lens up onto a ground-glass screen. Twin-lens reflex cameras suffer from PARALLAX error, particularly when focused at close distances, owing to the difference in position between the viewing lens and the taking lens. See also SINGLE-LENS REFLEX CAMERA.

Ultraviolet radiation. Electromagnetic radiation of wavelengths shorter than those of violet light, the shortest visible wavelength. They affect most photographic emulsions to some extent. See also INFRARED RADIATION.

Universal developer. Developing solutions for black-and-white materials that are intended for use with both films and printing papers.

Uprating. See PUSHING.

UV filter. Filter used over the camera lens to absorb ULTRAVIOLET RADIATION, which is particularly prevalent on hazy days. A UV filter enables the photographer to penetrate the haze to some extent.

Variable contrast paper. Photographic printing paper sensitized in such a way that it can give a range of different contrast grades. Each grade is activated by a different colored filter in the enlarger. The best-known paper of this sort is Ilford's MULTIGRADE. Multigrade's special emulsion has a mixture of two types of silver halide, one sensitive to blue light, the other to green light. Exposing the blue-sensitive part produces a high-contrast image; exposing the green-sensitive part produces a low-contrast image. Yellow filters are used to absorb blue light and transmit green, magenta filters to absorb green and transmit blue. An enlarger with a color-mixing head can be used with Multigrade paper, but greater control is possible with special Multigrade filters.

View camera. Large-format studio camera whose viewing system consists of a ground-glass screen at the back of the camera on which the picture is composed and focused before the film is inserted. The front and back of the camera are attached by a flexible bellows unit, which allows a full range of CAMERA MOVEMENTS.

Viewfinder. Window or frame on a camera, showing the scene that will appear in the picture, and often incorporating a RANGEFINDER.

Vignette. Picture printed in such a way that the image fades gradually into the border area.

Virtual image. In optics, an image that cannot be obtained on a screen; a virtual image is seen by an observer in a position through which rays of light appear to have passed, but in fact have not. See also REAL IMAGE.

Water softeners. Chemicals that remove or render harmless the calcium or magnesium salts present in 'hard' tap water. These impurities react with developers and may cause sum to be deposited on films.

Wavelength. The distance between successive points of equals 'phase' on a wave; the distance, for example, between successive crests or successive troughs.

Wetting agent. Chemical that has the effect of lowering the surface tension of water, often used in developers to prevent the formation of AIR BELLS, and in the final rinse (of film, in particular) to promote even drying.

Wide-angle lens. Lens of focal length shorter than that of a STANDARD LENS, and consequently having a wider ANGLE OF VIEW.

Working solution. Processing solution diluted to the strength at which it is intended to be used. Most chemicals are stored in a concentrated form, both to save space and to inhibit the deterioration of the chemical as a result of OXIDATION.

X-rays. Electromagnetic radiation with WAVELENGTHS very much shorter than those of visible light.

Zone focusing. Technique of presetting the aperture and focusing of the camera so that the entire zone in which the subject is likely to appear is covered by the DEPTH OF FIELD.

Zone system. System of relating exposure readings to tonal values in picture-taking, development and printing, popularized by the photographer Ansel Adams.

Zoom lens. Lens of variable FOCAL LENGTH whose focusing remains unchanged while its focal length is being altered. Zooming is accomplished by changing the relative positions of some of the elements within the lens.

KEEPING NOTES

Some people manage to work in the dark in complete chaos and still produce masterpieces. Most of us, however, can guarantee success only by working in a precise and organized fashion, taking infinite care over all the important details. It is not absolutely essential to make processing notes for every film, but doing so encourages an orderly way of working. Detailed notes also help you to perfect your technique, to correct faults and to make repeat prints without trial and error. On the following pages you will find forms on which you can record paper grades and sizes, exposure times, filtrations and any special notes relevant to a particular negative or print.

Negative file number				Contact sheet	
Film type					
Processing notes				Date	
Frame No.	Subject	Printing details			Derivations/ Notes
		Size	Paper	Exposure and filtration	

Negative file number				Contact sheet	
Film type					
Processing notes				Date	
Frame No.	Subject	Printing details			Derivations/ Notes
		Size	Paper	Exposure and filtration	

Negative file number				Contact sheet	
Film type					
Processing notes				Date	
Frame No.	Subject	Printing details			Derivations/ Notes
		Size	Paper	Exposure and filtration	

Negative file number				Contact sheet	
Film type					
Processing notes				Date	
Frame No.	Subject	Printing details			Derivations/ Notes
		Size	Paper	Exposure and filtration	

Negative file number				Contact sheet	
Film type					
Processing notes				Date	
Frame No.	Subject	Printing details			Derivations/ Notes
		Size	Paper	Exposure and filtration	

Negative file number			Contact sheet		
Film type					
Processing notes			Date		
Frame No.	Subject	Printing details			Derivations/ Notes
		Size	Paper	Exposure and filtration	

Negative file number				Contact sheet	
Film type					
Processing notes				Date	
Frame No.	Subject	Printing details			Derivations/ Notes
		Size	Paper	Exposure and filtration	

Negative file number				Contact sheet	
Film type					
Processing notes				Date	
Frame No.	Subject	Printing details			Derivations/ Notes
		Size	Paper	Exposure and filtration	

Negative file number				Contact sheet	
Film type					
Processing notes				Date	
Frame No.	Subject	Printing details			Derivations/ Notes
		Size	Paper	Exposure and filtration	

Negative file number				Contact sheet	
Film type					
Processing notes				Date	
Frame No.	Subject	Printing details			Derivations/ Notes
		Size	Paper	Exposure and filtration	

Negative file number				Contact sheet	
Film type					
Processing notes				Date	
Frame No.	Subject	Printing details			Derivations/ Notes
		Size	Paper	Exposure and filtration	

Negative file number				Contact sheet	
Film type					
Processing notes				Date	
Frame No.	Subject	Printing details			Derivations/ Notes
		Size	Paper	Exposure and filtration	

Negative file number				Contact sheet	
Film type					
Processing notes				Date	
Frame No.	Subject	Printing details			Derivations/ Notes
		Size	Paper	Exposure and filtration	

Negative file number				Contact sheet	
Film type					
Processing notes				Date	
Frame No.	Subject	Printing details			Derivations/ Notes
		Size	Paper	Exposure and filtration	

Negative file number			Contact sheet		
Film type					
Processing notes			Date		
Frame No.	Subject	Printing details			Derivations/ Notes
		Size	Paper	Exposure and filtration	

Negative file number				Contact sheet	
Film type					
Processing notes				Date	
Frame No.	Subject	Printing details			Derivations/ Notes
		Size	Paper	Exposure and filtration	

Negative file number			Contact sheet		
Film type					
Processing notes			Date		
Frame No.	Subject	Printing details			Derivations/ Notes
		Size	Paper	Exposure and filtration	

Negative file number				Contact sheet	
Film type					
Processing notes				Date	
Frame No.	Subject	Printing details			Derivations/ Notes
		Size	Paper	Exposure and filtration	

Negative file number				Contact sheet	
Film type					
Processing notes				Date	
Frame No.	Subject	Printing details			Derivations/ Notes
		Size	Paper	Exposure and filtration	

Negative file number				Contact sheet	
Film type					
Processing notes				Date	
Frame No.	Subject	Printing details			Derivations/ Notes
		Size	Paper	Exposure and filtration	

Negative file number				Contact sheet	
Film type					
Processing notes				Date	
Frame No.	Subject	Printing details			Derivations/ Notes
		Size	Paper	Exposure and filtration	

Negative file number				Contact sheet	
Film type					
Processing notes				Date	
Frame No.	Subject	Printing details			Derivations/ Notes
		Size	Paper	Exposure and filtration	

Negative file number				Contact sheet	
Film type					
Processing notes				Date	
Frame No.	Subject	Printing details			Derivations/ Notes
		Size	Paper	Exposure and filtration	

INDEX

Page numbers in **bold** type refer
to main entries.